PENNSYLVANIA TRIVIA

REVISED EDITION

PENNSYLVANIA TRIVIA

COMPILED BY ERNIE & JILL COUCH

REVISED EDITION

Rutledge Hill Press®
Nashville, Tennessee

A Division of Thomas Nelson, Inc.
www.ThomasNelson.com

Published by Rutledge Hill Press, a division of Thomas Nelson, Inc., P.O. Box 141000, Nashville, Tennessee 37214.

Typography by D&T/Bailey, Nashville, Tennessee

Library of Congress Cataloging-in-Publication Data

Couch, Ernie. 1949–
    Pennsylvania trivia / compiled by Ernie & Jill Couch.—Rev. ed.
      p. cm.
    ISBN 1-55853-356-7 (pbk.)
    1. Pennsylvania—Miscellanea.   I. Couch, Jill. 1948–   II. Title.
F149.5.C68   1995
974.8'0076—dc20   95-24376
                                                                                                            CIP

Printed in the United States of America

4 5 6 7 — 06 05 04

PREFACE

Pennsylvania stands at the forefront as a leader in the development of our great nation. The Commonwealth's colorful and compelling history speaks of a diversified land and people. Captured within these pages are some of the highlights of this rich heritage, both the well-known and the not-so-well-known.

This revised edition of *Pennsylvania Trivia* offers more than 150 new questions focusing on the Keystone State. *Pennsylvania Trivia* is designed to be informative, educational, and entertaining, and can be used with trivia format games. Most of all, we hope reading this book will motivate you to learn more about the great state of Pennsylvania and its people.

Ernie & Jill Couch

To
Sandra Abramson
and
the great people of Pennsylvania

TABLE OF CONTENTS

Geography 9

Entertainment 45

History 75

Arts & Literature 109

Sports & Leisure 135

Science & Nature 169

GEOGRAPHY

Q. The nation's first cloverleaf highway interchange was constructed in what Pennsylvania city?

A. Lima.

Q. Where was frontiersman Daniel Boone born in 1734?

A. Near Baumstown.

Q. What Westmoreland County community takes its name from the last syllables of the first and last names of one of the nation's first ladies?

A. Norvelt (for Eleanor Roosevelt).

Q. Where in 1868 was America's first beauty salon opened?

A. Philadelphia.

Q. Early settlers applied such names as Unionville, Skunk's Misery, and Slocum Hollow to what present-day Pennsylvania city?

A. Scranton.

Q. Near what town were Pennsylvania's first commercially culti-
vated mushrooms produced in 1904?

A. West Chester.

Q. By what name was Larksville called prior to 1895?

A. Blindtown.

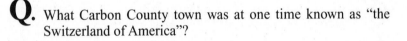

Q. Where was American painter Andrew Wyeth born in 1917?

A. Chadds Ford.

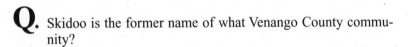

Q. What Carbon County town was at one time known as "the
Switzerland of America"?

A. Jim Thorpe (Maunch Chunk).

Q. Skidoo is the former name of what Venango County community?

A. Cherry Tree.

Q. What northwest Pennsylvania town controlled the world price
of oil for several years?

A. Oil City.

Q. What is the northernmost city in Pennsylvania?

A. Erie.

Q. What Susquehanna River community received its name from an early church steeple boatmen used for navigational reference?

A. Highspire.

Q. "Growing fat" is the meaning of what Indian place-name in Columbia County?

A. Catawissa.

Q. Where in 1853 was plate glass first manufactured?

A. Pittsburgh.

Q. The first Civil War battle fought north of the Mason-Dixon line took place on June 30, 1863, near what town?

A. Hanover.

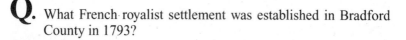

Q. What French royalist settlement was established in Bradford County in 1793?

A. French Azilum.

Q. Since 1810 what Luzerne County town has been known by such names as Scrabbletown, Skunktown, Coalville, Peestone, Hightown, Hendricksburg, Newton, Alberts, and Nanticoke Junction?

A. Ashley.

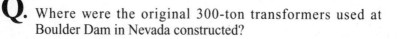

Q. Where were the original 300-ton transformers used at Boulder Dam in Nevada constructed?

A. Sharon.

Q. The design of what Pennsylvania city is very similar to that of Washington, DC?

A. Erie.

Q. What now defunct oil boomtown in Venango County grew from one family to 15,000 residents from May to September of 1865?

A. Pithole City.

Q. For whom was the University of Villanova named?

A. St. Thomas of Villanova, Bishop of Valencia.

Q. The Free Society of Traders, a land promotion company chartered by William Penn, gave its name to what original Philadelphia residential area?

A. Society Hill.

Q. What eighteenth-century British outpost fortification stood west of present-day Farmington?

A. Fort Necessity.

Q. What Monongahela River town is named in honor of the Revolutionary War general nicknamed the Swamp Fox?

A. Point Marion (for Francis Marion).

Q. What Pennsylvania city was named for two members of the British Parliament who sympathized with the colonists?

A. Wilkes-Barre (for John Wilkes and Isaac Barre).

Q. What name did William Penn first suggest for his North American grant?

A. New Wales.

Q. Where is John A. Sutter of California gold rush fame buried?

A. Lititz.

Q. What Perry County town founded in 1790 boasted seventeen inns during the canal boom era?

A. Millerstown.

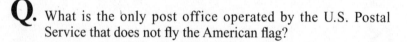

Q. What is the only post office operated by the U.S. Postal Service that does not fly the American flag?

A. B. Free Franklin Post Office and Museum (named after Franklin's unique signature-cancellation).

Q. What is the English translation of the Welsh place-name of Nanty Glo?

A. "Coal brook."

Q. What town lying between Pisgah Mountain and Broad Mountain was called "Hell's Kitchen" in its early days?

A. Nesquehoning.

Q. Welsh religious dissenter Rev. Rees Lloyd founded what Cambria County town?

A. Ebensburg.

Q. What Philadelphia thoroughfare is said to be the oldest residential street in the nation?

A. Elfreth's Alley.

Q. During the 1934 gubernatorial campaign where were five people shot to death and fourteen wounded during a Democratic parade?

A. Kelayres.

Q. What southwestern Pennsylvania community is the birthplace of baseball's Stan "the Man" Musial?

A. Donora.

Q. By what name did the early settlers refer to the site of Huntingdon?

A. Standing Stone.

Q. On September 11, 1777, Chadds Ford became the center of what Revolutionary War battle?

A. The Battle of Brandywine.

Q. What is the meaning of the Indian place-name Kittanning?

A. "Place of the great river."

Q. Where did Joseph Brown build a true polygon-shaped, twelve-sided house around 1860?

A. Near New Bedford.

Q. In what county did newspaper Horace Greeley establish a utopian communal colony in 1842?

A. Pike.

Q. The occasional shortage of water gave what early name to Mechanicsburg?

A. Drytown.

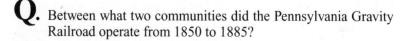

Q. Between what two communities did the Pennsylvania Gravity Railroad operate from 1850 to 1885?

A. Hawley and Scranton.

Q. Where was the first army Jeep built in 1940?

A. Butler.

Q. What Susquehanna River town was first called Wright's Ferry?

A. Columbia.

Q. In its early days, what Allegheny County town was called by such names as Fifetown, Dogtown, Contention, and Devil's Race Track?

A. Sewickley.

Q. What northern Tioga County community is named in honor of a War of 1812 naval hero?

A. Lawrenceville (for Capt. James Lawrence).

Q. "Meet me at the eagle," a familiar rendezvous designation in Philadelphia, refers to what bronze bird?

A. The one at John Wanamaker's department store.

Q. Where is the world's largest chocolate factory?

A. Hershey.

Q. What three different forts have stood at the present-day site of Franklin?

A. Fort Machault, Fort Venango, and Fort Franklin.

Q. Since 1911 what Mercer County town has carried the name of a one-time United States Steel Corporation president?

A. Farrell (for James A. Farrell).

Q. Where was militant abolitionist John Brown living when he finished formulating plans for his Harpers Ferry raid?

A. Chambersburg.

Q. The community of Angels is in the southern tip of what Pennsylvania county?

A. Wayne.

Q. Marcus Hook is a corruption of what Dutch name?

A. *Marretie's Hoeck.*

Q. Where was composer Stephen Collins Foster born on July 4, 1826?

A. Lawrenceville (now part of Pittsburgh).

Q. In what county in 1790 was the first iron furnace opened west of the Alleghenies?

A. Fayette.

Q. On what Pennsylvania river is the community of Skinners Eddy situated?

A. Susquehanna.

Q. The Anderson family of Lancaster conducts tours of one of the world's largest bakeries making what delicacy?

A. Pretzels.

Q. Where was the first screw factory in the nation constructed by Hardman Philips around 1820?

A. Philipsburg.

Q. Where do firefighters from many states attend classes throughout the year?

A. Pennsylvania Fire School, Lewistown.

Q. Where was the great steel industrialist Charles M. Schwab born in 1862?

A. Williamsburg.

Q. Early wagon drivers who had to use the bed of a shallow stream as a roadway led to the naming of what Pennsylvania community?

A. Water Street.

———◆———

Q. What community was established in Cambria County by the noted Catholic missionary Demetrius Augustine Gallitzin?

A. Loretto.

———◆———

Q. What girls' residential school was founded by Moravians in 1746?

A. Linden Hall, Lititz.

———◆———

Q. James Buchanan conducted his 1856 presidential campaign from the library of what mansion that he owned?

A. Wheatland, at Lancaster.

———◆———

Q. The name of Lake Winola in Wyoming County has what Indian meaning?

A. "Water lily."

———◆———

Q. Five thousand shingles was the price asked for the land on which what present-day Dauphin County community is situated?

A. Williamstown.

———◆———

Q. Prior to 1829, by what two names was Newport called?

A. Reider's Ferry and Reidersville.

Q. What was the northernmost point Confederate troops reached during the Civil War?

A. Lemoyne.

Q. What community in the southern Alleghenies is known as "the Town of Motels"?

A. Breezewood.

Q. Where was the world's first all-steel passenger train coach constructed in 1904?

A. Berwick.

Q. The abundance of wild hops gave what Susquehanna County community its name?

A. Hop Bottom.

Q. After Pittsburgh, what is Pennsylvania's busiest port?

A. Marcus Hook (twenty-fourth in the nation).

Q. What survey line completed in 1767 eventually became the accepted southern boundary of Pennsylvania?

A. Mason-Dixon.

Q. What town is considered "the Mushroom Capital of the World"?

A. Longwood.

Q. Where in 1684 did Rev. Thomas Dungan organize the first Baptist church in Pennsylvania?

A. Cold Spring.

———◆———

Q. What Lancaster County community is named in honor of the wife of Capt. Barnabas Hughes?

A. Elizabethtown.

———◆———

Q. Prior to 1846 by what name was Archbald called?

A. White Oak Run.

———◆———

Q. Where did glass and iron magnet Heinrich Wilhelm Stiegel construct his extravagant seventy-five-foot-high wooden castle in 1769?

A. Schaefferstown.

———◆———

Q. Pottsville is the location of what beer brewery, the oldest in the United States?

A. Yuengling.

———◆———

Q.  By what name was the site of Port Allegany known to the Indians?

A. "Canoe Place."

———◆———

Q. What Lackawanna County community is named for a wealthy English merchant?

A. Jermyn (for John Jermyn).

Q. What west Butler County community was laid out in 1835 by black freedman Thomas Baldwin?

A. Middle Lancaster.

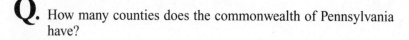

Q. Goshgoshing and Saqualingent are both former names of what Forest County community?

A. Tionesta.

Q. How many counties does the commonwealth of Pennsylvania have?

A. Sixty-seven.

Q. What company laid out Palmerton in 1898?

A. New Jersey Zinc.

Q. Where was the main intersection of Pennsylvania's north-south and east-west canal routes?

A. Amity Hall.

Q. What Luzerne County community received its name from the first forty settlers to locate in the area?

A. Forty Fort.

Q. The Phipps Conservatory in Pittsburgh's Shenley Park covers how many acres under glass?

A. 2.5.

Q. Poquessing Creek on the northeastern edge of Philadelphia proper is an Indian name of what meaning?

A. "Place of mice."

Q. Where was the U.S. Mint established in 1782?

A. Philadelphia.

Q. Where is Pauline's Trestle, upon which actress Pearl White was bound in the 1914 silent film serial *The Perils of Pauline*?

A. New Hope.

Q. For whom was Mansfield named?

A. Asa Mann.

Q. The community of Moon Run is in what county?

A. Allegheny.

Q. What western Pennsylvania fortification was completed in the spring of 1760 under the direction of General Stanwix?

A. Fort Pitt.

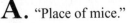

Q. Because of the variety of languages spoken by immigrant miners, by what early name was Duryea called?

A. Babel.

Q. Among the states, what is Pennsylvania's ranking according to population?

A. Fifth.

Q. In 1900 what eastern Pennsylvania community became the focal point of an artists' colony established by William Lathrop?

A. New Hope.

Q. For what railroad company surveyor was Lansdale named?

A. Phillip Lansdale Fox.

Q. Confederate troops occupied Chambersburg how many times during the Civil War?

A. Three.

Q. Where in 1876 was Alexander Graham Bell's telephone first publicly demonstrated?

A. The Philadelphia Centennial Exhibition.

Q. What is the largest natural lake wholly within the state?

A. Conneaut Lake, 3 miles long and 1.5 miles wide.

Q. The City of York is known by what symbol?

A. The white rose.

Q. What Delaware County facility is the oldest public building in continuous use in the nation?

A. The old Chester County Courthouse (built in 1724).

Q. What is the total area of Pennsylvania?

A. 45,126 square miles.

Q. The community of Sand Patch is in what county?

A. Somerset.

Q. In 1990, what percentage of Pennsylvania's population was classified as white?

A. 88.5 percent.

Q. When completed in 1902, what Pennsylvania railroad bridge was the longest stone-arch structure of its type in the nation?

A. The Rockville Bridge.

Q. What community was selected in the 1820s to serve as the seat of Perry County?

A. Bloomfield.

Q. Where was the Dorflinger Glass Works established in 1867?

A. White Mills.

Q. What Pennsylvania town was at one time nationally known as a major mart for horses used for pulling street-cars?

A. Mercer.

Q. Connellsville is situated on what river?

A. Youghiogheny.

Q. What Berks County town was laid out in 1742 on land owned by the Society of Jesus?

A. Bally.

Q. Where did the first autogiro flight take place in 1928?

A. Near Hatboro.

Q. What is the meaning of the Luzerne County Indian place-name of Shickshinny?

A. "Five mountains."

Q. Where was nineteenth-century multimillionaire coke and steel industrialist Henry Clay Frick born in 1849?

A. Scottsdale.

Q. Dr. William Smith, the first provost of the University of Pennsylvania, laid out what mid-Commonwealth town in 1767?

A. Huntingdon.

Q. What city calls itself "the Outlet Capital of the World"?

A. Reading.

Q. The Shawnee village of Obesson became the site of what present-day Mifflin County town?

A. Lewistown.

Q. The commonwealth of Pennsylvania is known by what nickname?

A. The Keystone State.

Q. Production of coal for consumption beyond local markets led to the name of what Westmoreland County community?

A. Export.

Q. What Philadelphia bridge crossing the Delaware River was the first in the nation to be named for a woman?

A. The Betsy Ross Bridge.

Q. During the Revolution, where was the Liberty Bell taken by wagon for safekeeping?

A. Zion's Church, Allentown.

Q. What Berks County community grew up around the King Solomon Tavern of the late 1700s?

A. Temple.

Q. From what college was James Buchanan, fifteenth president of the United States, expelled for engaging in "extravagance and mischief"?

A. Dickson.

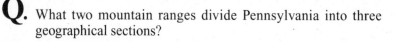

Q. What two mountain ranges divide Pennsylvania into three geographical sections?

A. Blue Ridge and Allegheny.

Q. Where in 1910 was rayon first commercially manufactured by the American Viscose Company?

A. Marcus Hook.

Q. The capitol dome, patterned after that of St. Peter's Cathedral in Rome, Italy, weighs how many pounds?

A. Fifty-two million.

Q. In 1849, what company founded Altoona?

A. The Pennsylvania Railroad, now Conrail, during construction of the first railroad over the Alleghenies.

Q. Founder Cyrus Blood named what Forest County community after his daughter?

A. Marienville.

Q. What Pennsylvania community is called "the Mail Order Capital of the United States"?

A. Hanover.

Q. Where in Pennsylvania may you visit one of the few Hindu temples in the United States?

A. Monroeville (Sri Venkateswara Temple).

Q. Where in 1839 was the first iron bridge west of the Alleghenies opened for service?

A. Brownsville.

Q. Why was Harrisburg named for John Harris?

A. He refused to sell needed land to the legislature until the name was changed from Louisborg, for Louis XVI.

Q. How many covered bridges dot southwestern Pennsylvania's Washington and Greene Counties?

A. Thirty-five.

Q. For what early proponent of the public school system and mining engineer is Lansford named?

A. Asa Lansford Foster.

Q. On top of what promontory was the colonial fortification of Fort Henry constructed?

A. Round Head.

Q. What Pennsylvania suburb is named for the home of George Fox, the founder of the Society of Friends?

A. Swarthmore (for Swarthmore Hall).

Q. The corruption of Indian words describing locally large swarms of gnats created what Jefferson County place-name?

A. Punxsutawney.

Q. On what date did Pennsylvania gain statehood?

A. December 12, 1787.

Q. What Lancaster County community bears the old name of the biblical town of Bethlehem?

A. Ephrata.

Q. What body of water forms a portion of Pennsylvania's northern boundary?

A. Lake Erie.

Q. Where is the U.S. brig *Niagara,* used by Como. Oliver Hazard Perry to defeat the british in 1813, moored?

A. Erie.

Q. During the Devil War where was Camp Curtin established?

A. Harrisburg.

Q. What is unusual about a Pennsylvania town name of Hamlin?

A. There are two of them: east of Scranton and north of Lebanon.

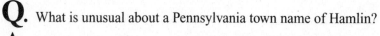

Q. Soloman Spaulding, who wrote *The Manuscript Found,* believed by some to be the basis of the *Book of Mormon*, is buried in what southwest Pennsylvania community?

A. Amity.

Q. What Indian village at one time occupied the present site of Williamsport?

A. French Margaret's Town.

Q. Yankeetown was the former name of what southern Clinton County community?

A. Lamar.

Q. The old adage "A bird in the hand is worth two in the bush," illustrated on an early tavern sign, led to the naming of what Pennsylvania community?

A. Bird-in-Hand.

Q. By what name was Dunmore called until 1840?

A. Buckstown.

Q. Because of its large number of buggy manufacturers what Union County town was nicknamed "Buggytown, USA"?

A. Mifflinburg.

Q. Butlers Mill was the former name of what eastern Pennsylvania community?

A. Chalfont.

Q. James G. Blaine, who almost defeated Grover Cleveland in 1884 for the presidency, was born in what Monogahela River town in 1830?

A. West Brownsville.

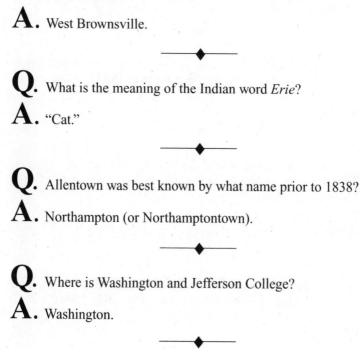

Q. What is the meaning of the Indian word *Erie*?

A. "Cat."

Q. Allentown was best known by what name prior to 1838?

A. Northampton (or Northamptontown).

Q. Where is Washington and Jefferson College?

A. Washington.

Q. What house museum in Upland is the only remaining house known to have been visited by William Penn?

A. The Caleb Pusey House on Landingford Plantation.

Q. The former site of the Indian village of Killiman is now the location of what Pittsburgh suburb?

A. Crafton.

Q. Where was writer Louisa May Alcott born in 1832?

A. Germantown.

Q. What distance separates the northern and southern borders of Pennsylvania?

A. 169 miles.

Q. Where did Thomas A. Edison construct the world's first three-wire incandescent lighting power plant in 1883?

A. Sunbury.

Q. The establishment of an axe factory in 1828 by Harvey Mann and William Mann Jr. led to the naming of what Centre County community?

A. Axemann.

Q. The merging of the Appalachian Ridge and Valley region and the Appalachian Plateau forms what geographical area?

A. The Allegheny Front.

Q. What area in southern Pennsylvania has the highest point of elevation in the state?

A. Mount Davis in Somerset County (3,213 feet above sea level).

Q. "The Gem City" refers to what Pennsylvania metropolis?

A. Erie.

Q. What town is situated at the confluence of the Susquehanna and Chemung Rivers?

A. Athens.

Q. In what county is the geographic center of the state?

A. Centre County.

———◆———

Q. What is the largest county in the Commonwealth?

A. Lycoming (1,237 square miles).

———◆———

Q. Where was inventor Robert Fulton born on November 14, 1765?

A. Near Little Britain, Lancaster County.

———◆———

Q. Where is the lowest elevation in Pennsylvania?

A. Along the Delaware River (sea level).

———◆———

Q. What mountains in the northeastern part of the state are part of the Appalachian Plateau?

A. Pocono.

———◆———

Q. At what cities does the Ohio River begin and end?

A. Pittsburgh (where the Allegheny and Monogahela Rivers meet) and Cairo, Illinois (where it flows into the Mississippi River).

———◆———

Q. What town is named for the 1779–83 French minister to America?

A. Luzerne (for Chevalier de la Luzerne).

Q. Where was the state capital from 1799 until 1812?

A. Lancaster.

———◆———

Q. What Indiana County community received its name from being on a mountain top?

A. Nolo (no low ground).

———◆———

Q. Where did Rabbi Joseph Kranskopf of Philadelphia establish the National Farm School in 1896?

A. Near Doylestown.

———◆———

Q. Where in 1683 was Pennsylvania's first glassmaking enterprise established?

A. Frankford (now a part of Philadelphia).

———◆———

Q. What Schuylkill County town's name is an Indian word meaning "beaver"?

A. Tamaqua.

———◆———

Q. In the 1950s, what town was formed by joining Mauch Chunk and East Mauch Chunk?

A. Jim Thorpe.

———◆———

Q. What Pennsylvania bay played an important role in the construction and protection of Oliver Hazard Perry's fleet during his Lake Erie campaign in 1813?

A. Presque Isle Bay.

Q. What is the greatest distance between the eastern and western borders of Pennsylvania?

A. 307 miles.

Q. What Blair County town was settled in 1850 by North Ireland immigrants and given the Irish name meaning "the land of Owen"?

A. Tyrone.

Q. During the early 1800s Jersey Shore was known by what name?

A. Waynesburg.

Q. Pittsburgh's wedge-shaped business district between its two rivers has what name?

A. The Golden Triangle.

Q. A major cave-in of underlying mine tunnels on March 4, 1940, caused extensive damage to homes in a sixteen-block area of what Schuylkill County town?

A. Shenandoah.

Q. Which Pennsylvania county is known as "the Buckwheat County"?

A. Butler.

Q. Where in 1892 did the Textile Machine Works establish itself as the nation's first manufacturer of braiding and knitting machines?

A. Wyomissing.

Q. Where was the 1880 Democratic presidential candidate Winfield Scott Hancock born?

A. Montgomery Square.

Q. What Mifflin County community was previously known as Freedom Forge and Logan?

A. Burnham.

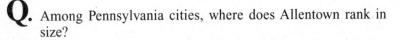

Q. By what name was Center Square known prior to 1758?

A. Wagon.

Q. Among Pennsylvania cities, where does Allentown rank in size?

A. Fourth.

Q. What stream serves as the dividing line between East Stroudsburg and Stroudsburg?

A. Broadhead's Creek.

Q. Covering thirteen square miles, what is the largest body of water in Pennsylvania?

A. Artificially created Raystown Lake.

Q. What is the origin of the name of the town of Intercourse?

A. Either entrance to the old racecourse (Entercourse) close to the town, or the joining (intercourse) of the Old King's Highway and the Wilmington-Erie Road.

Q. Towanda, which is an Indian place-name meaning "where we bury the dead," was known by what prior name?

A. Meansville.

Q. What counties make up the Endless Mountains region?

A. Bradford, Sullivan, Susquehanna, and Wyoming.

Q. By what name was Blossburg first called?

A. Peters Camp.

Q. Where was the famous Revolutionary War–era painter Benjamin West born?

A. Swarthmore.

Q. What is the state's leading manufacturing activity?

A. Food processing.

Q. Norriton Plantation and Mill Tract are both former names of what southeastern Pennsylvania city?

A. Norristown.

Q. What river forms the eastern boundary of Pennsylvania?

A. Delaware.

Q. In 1900 what Pennsylvania city became the first major city in the world to install a completely underground telephone line system?

A. Philadelphia.

Q. What famous Pennsylvania Dutch country pastry has a filling of molasses and brown sugar?

A. Shoofly pie.

Q. What three states beside Pennsylvania are called Commonwealths?

A. Kentucky, Massachusetts, and Virginia.

—◆—

Q. Dickinson College is in what community?

A. Carlisle.

—◆—

Q. Where does Pennsylvania rank in geographic size among the other states?

A. Thirty-third.

—◆—

Q. How much anthracite (hard coal) produced in the United States comes from Pennsylvania?

A. All of it.

Q. The Governor's Mansion in Harrisburg overlooks what river?

A. Susquehanna.

Q. Near what Pennsylvania town were iron plates fabricated for the famous Union ironclad the *Monitor*?

A. Coatesville, at Laurel Forge.

———◆———

Q. Where on exhibit is Loretto, the private railroad car of steel baron Charles M. Schwab?

A. Railroaders Memorial Museum, Altoona.

———◆———

Q. Where was the first glass works west of the Allegheny Mountains established by Albert Gallatin after the Revolutionary War?

A. New Geneva.

———◆———

Q. Originally called Blue Rocks, what southeastern Pennsylvania community was renamed in honor of the one-time publisher of the Philadelphia *Inquirer*?

A. Elverson.

———◆———

Q. Tom Quick in 1733 became the first settler of what Pike County community?

A. Milford.

———◆———

Q. What seven-story structure stands atop Mount Penn overlooking the city of Reading?

A. The Pagoda.

———◆———

Q. What two Pennsylvania rivers serve as major tributaries to the Delaware?

A. Lehigh and Schuylkill.

Q. How many votes does Pennsylvania have in the Electoral College?

A. Twenty-one.

———◆———

Q. What were the three original counties in Pennsylvania?

A. Bucks, Chester, and Philadelphia.

———◆———

Q. Where did George Washington assemble his troops just prior to crossing the Delaware to capture Trenton on Christmas night 1776?

A. Concentration Valley.

———◆———

Q. Scottsdale, named in honor of Pennsylvania Railroad president Thomas A. Scott, was originally known by what name?

A. Fountain Mills.

———◆———

Q. Maguntchi and Salzburg are both former names of what Lehigh County town?

A. Emmaus.

———◆———

Q. What community on Red Bank Creek was at one time called Gumtown?

A. New Bethlehem.

———◆———

Q. Where did the grandsons of noted gunmaker William Henry manufacture firearms until 1904?

A. Belfast.

Q. Where on July 17, 1856, did two trains collide head-on, resulting in sixty deaths and more than one hundred injuries?

A. Ambler.

———◆———

Q. Their ancestral home in England provided Thomas and Richard Penn, sons of William Penn, with the name for what Pennsylvania city?

A. Reading.

———◆———

Q. How many states share a border with the commonwealth of Pennsylvania?

A. Six (Ohio, West Virginia, Maryland, Delaware, New Jersey, and New York).

———◆———

Q. What is the meaning of the name of the Moravian settlement of Friedenshutten, which was situated near present-day Browntown Mountain?

A. "Tents of peace."

———◆———

Q. What house in New Castle served as an important regional station on the Underground Railroad?

A. The White Homestead.

———◆———

Q. Settled in 1792, what southeastern Indiana County community received an Irish name meaning "field on a hill"?

A. Armagh.

———◆———

Q. What fortification was constructed at the mouth of Fishing Creek on the Susquehanna River in 1756?

A. Fort Hunter.

Q. Where was the *Codorus,* the nation's first wood-burning iron steamboat, constructed?

A. York.

Q. Where in 1851 was the first blood shed in connection with the Fugitive Slave Law?

A. Christiana.

Q. California State University is in what Pennsylvania county?

A. Washington County.

Q. The two-phased Pennamite-Yankee War was brought on by settlers from what state trying to establish themselves in the Wyoming Valley on behalf of their home state?

A. Connecticut.

Q. What Bucks County community has a name that is Indian for "great mountain"?

A. Lahaska.

Q. What Potter County town is named for an Amsterdam banking executive?

A. Coudersport (for Jean Samuel Coudere).

Q. Of what ethnic background are the Pennsylvania Dutch?

A. German (the word *Dutch* is a mispronunciation of *Deutsch,* meaning "German").

Q. What Snyder County community is named for a nineteenth-century journalist, politician, and author?

A. McClure (for Alexander Kelly McClure).

Q. At one time the largest steel coal tipple in the world was in what Somerset County community?

A. Boswell (1,200 feet long and 120 feet high).

Q. Picturesque Buchanan Valley is in what land region?

A. The Blue Ridge.

Q. Northampton occupies the site of what former Indian village?

A. Hokendauqua.

Q. Tavern, sawmill, and distillery owner Thomas Reed founded what town in 1793?

A. Minersville.

Q. What Pennsylvania city was named after William Penn's father-in-law's Northamptonshire estate?

A. Waston (for Easton-Weston).

Q. How many international airports are in Pennsylvania?

A. Six (Allentown, Erie, Harrisburg, Philadelphia, Pittsburgh, Wilkes-Barre/Scranton).

Q. Where was Thiel College founded in 1866 through a donation by Pittsburgh businessman A. Louis Thiel?

A. Greenville.

Q. What is the seat of Cameron County?

A. Emporium.

Q. For whom did founder Robert Humphrey name the community of West Alexander in 1796?

A. His wife (Martha Alexander Humphrey).

Q. The community of Boot Jack is in what county?

A. Elk.

Q. When settled in 1682, Darby was known by what name?

A. Derbytown.

Q. "Hill by the waters" is the meaning of what Scottish-named Pittsburgh suburb?

A. Ben Avon.

Q. Exiled Polish nobleman Francis Helvedi established what Pennsylvania town in 1813?

A. Monaca.

ENTERTAINMENT

Q. In 1905 the first Nickelodeon theater opened its doors in Pittsburgh showing what eleven-minute movie?

A. *The Great Train Robbery.*

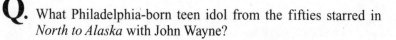

Q. In 1957 Phoenixville-born composer Terry Gilkyson wrote and recorded with the East Riders what million-selling Calypso hit?

A. "Marianne."

Q. Lancaster provided the setting for what Oscar-winning 1985 film?

A. *Witness.*

Q. What female country music artist was born in Bloomsburg?

A. Lacy J. Dalton.

Q. What Philadelphia-born teen idol from the fifties starred in *North to Alaska* with John Wayne?

A. Fabian.

Q. *Your Show of Shows* combined the talents of Sid Caesar with what Philadelphia-born comedienne?

A. Imogene Coca.

Q. Pittsburgh native David Lewis won an Emmy Award for outstanding supporting actor in 1982 while on what daytime drama serial?

A. *General Hospital.*

Q. What Philadelphia-formed recording duo first reached number one on the charts with "Rich Girl"?

A. Hall and Oates (Daryl Hall and John Oates).

Q. Pitcairn, near Pittsburgh, was the birthplace of what Big Band orchestra leader?

A. Ted Weems.

Q. CBS filmed what 1978 television project for its *American Classic* series in Jim Thorpe?

A. "You Can't Go Home Again."

Q. Bill Cosby hosted what children's cartoon show with characters created from his Philadelphia childhood?

A. *Fat Albert and the Cosby Kids.*

Q. In what Pennsylvania community was the 1983 movie *Maria's Lovers* filmed?

A. Brownsville.

Q. What television show that began in Philadelphia in 1952 became ABC's longest running series?

A. *American Bandstand.*

———◆———

Q. What Johnstown-born actress portrayed Luz Benedict II, a daughter of Bick Benedict (Rock Hudson), in the film classic *Giant*?

A. Carroll Baker.

———◆———

Q. In 1961, what Philadelphia rock'n'roll group had a number two hit with "Bristol Stomp"?

A. The Dovells.

———◆———

Q. In what Pennsylvania community was veteran actor Jimmy Stewart born?

A. Indiana.

———◆———

Q. Marian the Librarian was portrayed by Smithton native Shirley Jones in what Meredith Willson musical film?

A. *The Music Man.*

———◆———

Q. What well-known New Hope theater is situated in a mill dating from the 1780s?

A. Bucks County Playhouse.

———◆———

Q. Where is the Great Pumpkin Weekend, featuring foods made from pumpkins, held the last weekend in October?

A. John Chads House, Chadds Ford.

Q. Philadelphia's JFK Stadium was the site of what 1985 rock concert, the world's largest to date?

A. LIVE-AID.

◆

Q. What Pittsburgh-born actress played Agent 99 in the television spy spoof *Get Smart*?

A. Barbara Feldon.

◆

Q. What seasonal lighting display in Bernville has become one of the top ten travel attractions in Pennsylvania?

A. Koziar's Christmas Village.

◆

Q. What television show was the only major national series to originate from Philadelphia from 1965 to 1978?

A. *The Mike Douglas Show.*

◆

Q. Justin DeRosa, formerly of Lawrence County, became a success at what profession in Hollywood?

A. Stuntman.

◆

Q. What Philadelphia-born Big Band singer had hits in 1954 with "Little Things Mean a Lot" and "In the Chapel in the Moonlight"?

A. Kitty Kallen.

◆

Q. What Pennsylvania community served as the location for the 1983 Tom Cruise movie *All the Right Moves*?

A. Johnstown.

Q. In the early 1900s, what Philadelphia optician set up a studio in Betzwood where some of the country's first feature-length motion pictures were produced?

A. Sigmund Lubin.

———◆———

Q. In what Pennsylvania community did disc jockey Alan Freed first work in radio?

A. New Castle (WKST).

———◆———

Q. Philadelphia native David Mann is best known for what 1941 hit song?

A. "There! I've Said It Again."

———◆———

Q. Pennsylvania native Lionel Barrymore portrayed what character in the Christmas classic *It's a Wonderful Life*?

A. Mr. Potter, the banker.

———◆———

Q. What Pittsburgh native portrayed the character Draper Scott on the TV soap opera *The Edge of Night*?

A. Tony Craig.

———◆———

Q. Longtime Philadelphia resident Dick Clark received an Emmy Award in 1979 for hosting what television game show?

A. *The $20,000 Pyramid.*

———◆———

Q. What Pittsburgh-based group recorded its only major hit, "See You in September," in 1959?

A. The Tempos.

Q. At what amusement center may one enjoy a waterfall plunge considered to be the world's tallest?

A. Dorney Park and Wildwater Kingdom, near Allentown.

Q. What Philadelphian was the first black actor to star in a television dramatic/adventure series?

A. Bill Cosby (*I Spy,* 1965).

Q. Michael McKean and David L. Lander, Lenny and Squiggy of the *Laverne and Shirley* show, attended what Pennsylvania university?

A. Carnegie Mellon University.

Q. In 1984, what Pittsburgh native won an Oscar as Best Actor for his role in *Amadeus*?

A. F. Murray Abraham.

Q. Philadelphia native Sidney Lumet directed what 1982 thriller starring Michael Caine and Christopher Reeve?

A. *Deathtrap.*

Q. Lyricist Oscar Hammerstein II died in what Pennsylvania community in 1960?

A. Doylestown.

Q. What Harrisburg-born actor portrayed Sergeant Gorman in the 1970 movie M*A*S*H?

A. Bobby Troup.

Q. What Philadelphia landmark department store was used in filming the 1986 romantic comedy *Mannequin*?

A. John Wanamaker's.

Q. Philadelphia-born Hugh Marlowe played accountant Jim Matthews on what daytime drama serial?

A. *Another World.*

Q. What New Castle native portrayed George Kerby on the CBS sitcom *Topper*?

A. Robert Sterling.

Q. Nancy Hamilton, a Sewickley native, is best remembered as the lyricist for what 1940 song?

A. "How High the Moon."

Q. What famous swimmer and actor from Windber portrayed Tarzan in the movie series?

A. Johnny Weissmuller.

Q. In 1955 what Philadelphia male singing group recorded the number one national hit, "Love Is a Many Splendored Thing"?

A. The Four Aces.

Q. What Pittsburgh-born actor became famous for his role as retired detective Nick Charles in the crime-comedy series of *Thin Man* films?

A. William Powell.

Q. Producers Kenny Gamble and Leon Huff remade Philadelphia into a soul capital in the mid-seventies by establishing what recording label?

A. Philadelphia International.

Q. In what television show did Philadelphia native Henry Jones play the role of Judge Jonathan Dexter?

A. *Phyllis.*

Q. For what movie did Chester-born blues singer and actress Ethel Waters receive an Academy Award nomination for a role that she translated from Broadway to Hollywood?

A. *A Member of the Wedding.*

Q. At what Pennsylvania instructional institution was the 1981 movie *Taps* filmed?

A. The Valley Forge Military Academy.

Q. What Scranton-born lyricist created such songs as "When You Wish upon a Star" and "High Noon"?

A. Ned Washington.

Q. Easton became famous for what product enjoyed by children worldwide?

A. Crayola crayons.

Q. What Philadelphia rocker had a 1983 national hit with "Escalator of Life"?

A. Robert Hazard.

Q. Annette Funicello co-starred with what Philadelphia-born rock'n'roll singer in the "beach" films of the early 1960s?

A. Frankie Avalon.

◆

Q. What Pennsylvania-born actor hosted the ABC series *Ripley's Believe It or Not?*

A. Jack Palance.

◆

Q. Trafford-born actress Lauren Tewes portrayed what character on ABC's *The Love Boat?*

A. Julie McCoy, the ship's cruise director.

◆

Q. Pittsburgh native Charles Grodin became romantically involved with Miss Piggy in what 1981 film?

A. *The Great Muppet Caper.*

◆

Q. What was Philadelphia-born Eddie Fisher's first million-selling record?

A. "Any Time" (1951).

◆

Q. As of 1995, how many Miss America titleholders hailed from Pennsylvania?

A. Five (1924, 1935, 1936, 1939, 1954).

◆

Q. What Philadelphia-born musician played in the bands of Stan Kenton, Jimmy Dorsey, Benny Goodman, and Woody Herman before forming his own group in 1949?

A. Stan Getz.

Q. Brothers Jimmy and Tommy Dorsey, both Big Band leaders, were born in what Pennsylvania town?

A. Shenandoah.

Q. What Philadelphian was named Las Vegas Entertainer of the Year in 1977?

A. David Brenner.

Q. What Pittsburgh native provided the orchestra for the long-running *Carol Burnett Show*?

A. Peter Matz.

Q. In what community was the 1987 movie *Tiger Warsaw* filmed, starring Patrick Swayze?

A. Sharon.

Q. Philadelphian Broderick Crawford starred as Capt. Dan Mathews in what television crime show?

A. *Highway Patrol.*

Q. What Pittsburgh-born comedian established a solo act in 1968 after teaming with Steve Rossi for several years?

A. Marty Allen.

Q. What Philadelphia group recorded the 1958 hit "Rock and Roll Is Here to Stay"?

A. Danny and the Juniors.

Q. What South Philadelphia-born concert singer received the Presidential Medal of Freedom in 1963?

A. Marian Anderson.

Q. Jennifer Beals played Alex, a go-go dancer, in what 1983 movie filmed in Pittsburgh?

A. *Flashdance.*

Q. In what 1952 MGM musical did Pittsburgh native Gene Kelly star with Donald O'Connor and Debbie Reynolds?

A. *Singin' in the Rain.*

Q. What Canonsburg-born singer/musician had his first national hit with the 1962 recording of "Roses Are Red"?

A. Bobby Vinton.

Q. Blake Carrington's attorney, Andy Laird, was played by what Philadelphia-born actor on ABC's *Dynasty*?

A. Peter Mark Richman.

Q. What Philadelphia-born actress portrayed public defender Joyce Davenport in the television crime series *Hill Street Blues*?

A. Veronica Hamel.

Q. The Pennsylvania Maple Festival held in Meyersdale each spring features what pageant?

A. *Legend of the Magic Water.*

Q. Sharon-born actor Lester Rawlins portrayed the character Orin Hillyer in what television soap opera?

A. *The Edge of Night.*

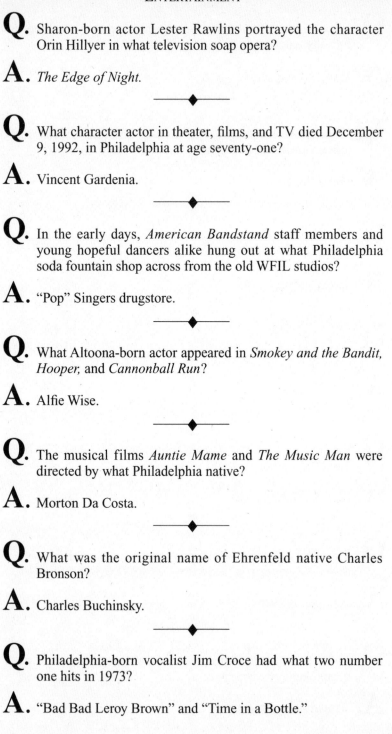

Q. What character actor in theater, films, and TV died December 9, 1992, in Philadelphia at age seventy-one?

A. Vincent Gardenia.

Q. In the early days, *American Bandstand* staff members and young hopeful dancers alike hung out at what Philadelphia soda fountain shop across from the old WFIL studios?

A. "Pop" Singers drugstore.

Q. What Altoona-born actor appeared in *Smokey and the Bandit, Hooper,* and *Cannonball Run*?

A. Alfie Wise.

Q. The musical films *Auntie Mame* and *The Music Man* were directed by what Philadelphia native?

A. Morton Da Costa.

Q. What was the original name of Ehrenfeld native Charles Bronson?

A. Charles Buchinsky.

Q. Philadelphia-born vocalist Jim Croce had what two number one hits in 1973?

A. "Bad Bad Leroy Brown" and "Time in a Bottle."

Q. "J.T." a 1969 CBS *Children's Hour* drama set in Harlem, starred what two Philadelphia natives?

A. Janet DuBois and Kevin Hooks.

———◆———

Q. What longtime resident of Canton was famous during the 1800s for his stage characterization of Davy Crockett?

A. Frank Mayo.

———◆———

Q. The NBC sitcom *Amen* starred what Philadelphia-born actor as Deacon Frye?

A. Sherman Hemsley.

———◆———

Q. In what television western did Pennsylvania native Cameron Mitchell play the character Buck Cannon?

A. *High Chaparral.*

———◆———

Q. What Philadelphia-based group had its first national hit in 1962 with "The Wah Watusi"?

A. The Orlons.

———◆———

Q. Comedian Ernie Kovacs was married to what Kingston-born singer/actress?

A. Edie Adams.

———◆———

Q. What Pittsburgh-born producer received two Emmy Awards (1966 and 1967) for his achievements on *The Andy Williams Show*?

A. Robert "Bob" Finkel.

Q. Canonsburg-born Perry Como was established in what career before becoming a professional singer?

A. Barbering.

Q. Philadelphia native Steven Kampmann portrayed what character on TV's *Newhart*?

A. Kirk Devane, the compulsive liar who ran the cafe next door.

Q. What Philadelphia-born actor portrayed Chuck Colson in the CBS docudrama on Watergate, "Blind Ambition"?

A. Michael Callan.

Q. Charleroi native Barbara Bosson played what character on the crime show *Hill Street Blues*?

A. Fay Furillo (Frank's ex-wife).

Q. What Pittsburgh native wrote the 1930s song "Beyond the Blue Horizon"?

A. Leo Robin.

Q. Philadelphia-born actress Audrey Landers portrayed singer Afton Cooper on what prime time serial?

A. *Dallas.*

Q. What ABC sitcom was built around a Philadelphia waitress who married a wealthy pediatrician?

A. *Angie.*

Q. What famous Tyrone-born musician directed The Pennsylvanians for more than sixty years?

A. Fred Waring.

Q. Philadelphian Jack Whitaker hosted what CBS children's series broadcast from the Philadelphia Zoo?

A. *Meet Me at the Zoo.*

Q. McDonald native Jay Livingston received an Oscar for what 1956 composition?

A. "Que Sera Sera."

Q. What Philadelphia-born actress formed a comedy team with Mike Nichols?

A. Elaine May.

Q. Scenes from what movie were filmed on Route 985 close to Jennerstown?

A. *Slapshot.*

Q. What Canonsburg-based group had a 1955 double-sided hit with "Maybe" and "I Love You Madly"?

A. The Four Coins.

Q. Officer Jim Corrigan on the ABC series *T. J. Hooker* was played by what Philadelphia-born actor?

A. James Darren.

Q. What 1985 movie about two buddies from South Philadelphia starred Nicolas Cage and Matthew Modine?

A. *Birdy.*

Q. *TV's Top Tunes,* a 1954 summer replacement for *The Perry Como Show,* was hosted by what Bentleyville-born orchestra leader?

A. Ray Anthony.

Q. South Philadelphia native Joseph Roman played what character on the NBC crime show *Quincy*?

A. Sergeant Brill.

Q. In 1940, Pennsylvanian James Stewart won an Oscar for what film also starring Katharine Hepburn and Cary Grant?

A. *Philadelphia Story.*

Q. What Pennsylvania-born actress portrayed Jane Hathaway on the *Beverly Hillbillies*?

A. Nancy Kulp.

Q. In what 1956 film did Philadelphia-born actress Grace Kelly star with Frank Sinatra and Bing Crosby?

A. *High Society.*

Q. What Philadelphia native is credited with establishing the use of the Hammond electric organ in rhythm and blues?

A. Bill Doggett.

Q. Philadelphia-born actor Jack Klugman portrayed what character in the Emmy Award-winning sitcom *The Odd Couple*?

A. Oscar Madison.

Q. What is the real name of country music artist Lacy J. Dalton?

A. Jill Byrem.

Q. Haverford provided the setting for what 1983 movie starring Tom Berenger and Michael Paré?

A. *Eddie and the Cruisers.*

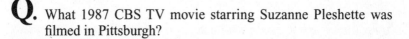

Q. What 1987 CBS TV movie starring Suzanne Pleshette was filmed in Pittsburgh?

A. *Command in Hell.*

Q. What 1935 hit film began a longtime professional association for soprano Jeanette MacDonald, a Philadelphia native, and baritone Nelson Eddy?

A. *Naughty Marietta.*

Q. What 1983 comedy filmed in Philadelphia starred Eddie Murphy as a con man and Dan Aykroyd as a snobbish commodities broker?

A. *Trading Places.*

Q. Teddy Pendergrass sang lead for what Philadelphia-based singing group from 1970 to 1976?

A. Harold Melvin & the Blue Notes.

Q. From 1963 to 1990, Pittsburgh-born actor Regis Toomey portrayed Doc Stuart on what CBS rural sitcom?

A. *Petticoat Junction.*

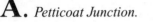

Q. In 1982 what Philadelphia-born singer/guitarist had a number one hit with the single "I Love Rock'n'Roll"?

A. Joan Jett.

Q. What Philadelphia-born actor appeared with Don Knotts in *The Ghost and Mr. Chicken* and *How to Frame a Figg*?

A. Eddie Quillan.

Q. Rock legend Bruce Springsteen won four Grammy Awards in 1995 for what song of his?

A. "Streets of Philadelphia."

Q. Reading-born actor Forrest Compton was featured in what role on the television show *Gomer Pyle, U.S.M.C.*?

A. Colonel Gray, the commanding officer.

Q. What Pittsburgh native produced such movie classics as *Top Hat, Hunchback of Notre Dame, National Velvet,* and *A Patch of Blue*?

A. Pandro S. Berman.

Q. Swan Records of Philadelphia produced what 1959 smash hit by Freddy Cannon?

A. "Tallahassee Lassie" (written by his mother).

Q. Pennsylvanian Edward Binns portrayed what character on the CBS drama series *The Nurses*?

A. Dr. Kiley.

Q. What South Philly-born tenor became internationally known in film, in opera, and for such recordings as "Be My Love"?

A. Mario Lanza.

Q. Shot on location, what 1980 movie portrayed John Travolta as a sound man for a Philadelphia movie factory?

A. *Blow Out.*

Q. What world-famous parade in Philadelphia starts off the New Year?

A. Mummers' Parade.

Q. Duquesne-born jazz performer Earl "Fatha" Hines became internationally known for his talents on what instrument?

A. Piano.

Q. Ernest Evans, who in high school worked as a chicken plucker in a Philadelphia poultry shop, later popularized the Twist using what name?

A. Chubby Checker.

Q. Actor Cameron Mitchell was born in what York County community?

A. Dallastown.

Q. What nickname was given to studio musicians who played on most of the Sound of Philadelphia records released by Philadelphia International Records?

A. MFSB (Mother, Father, Sister, Brother).

◆

Q. Harrisburgh-born Richard Sanders portrayed what character on *WKRP in Cincinnati*?

A. Les Nesman, the station's newsman.

◆

Q. What movie shot in Pittsburgh won the 1978 Academy Award for Best Picture?

A. *The Deer Hunter.*

◆

Q. "Long Lonely Nights" and "Tear Drops" were national hits by what Philadelphia-based late-1950s male singing group?

A. Lee Andrews and The Hearts.

◆

Q. What 1984 science fiction thriller movie was built around a supposed 1943 government experiment at the Philadelphia Navy Yard?

A. *The Philadelphia Experiment.*

◆

Q. The television comedy-drama *Room 222* featured what Reading-born actor as principal Seymour Kaufman?

A. Michael Constantine.

◆

Q. What Philadelphia eatery is a virtual museum of aged paneling and Currier and Ives lithographs?

A. Bookbinders Old Original.

Q. Philadelphia-born singer Al Martino sold more than a million copies of what 1965 hit?

A. "Spanish Eyes."

Q. What Scranton-born singer/actor appeared in such films as *Moonlight in Havana, Crazy Horse,* and *The Singing Sheriff?*

A. Allan Jones.

Q. In 1905 where in Pennsylvania was the first theater opened solely for the purpose of showing motion pictures?

A. Pittsburgh.

Q. In 1974 what Philadelphia-based group was the first black band ever to play New York's Metropolitan Opera House?

A. Labelle.

Q. In what 1970s television detective series did Philadelphian Nancy Walker appear as the housekeeper?

A. *McMillan and Wife.*

Q. "Queen of the Yodelers" was the title given to what Old Forge native in the 1940s and 1950s?

A. Rosalie Allen.

Q. What Shenandoah native directed such television sitcoms as *Get Smart, Bewitched,* and *McHale's Navy?*

A. Sidney Miller.

Q. In what movie did the Philadelphia Orchestra become the first symphonic group to appear in a major motion picture?

A. *The Big Broadcast of 1937.*

Q. Sylvester Stallone scaled the steps of what Philadelphia institution in *Rocky* (1978)?

A. The Philadelphia Museum of Art.

Q. What Pennsylvania-born actress portrayed the wife of Henry Fonda in the ABC comedy-drama *The Smith Family*?

A. Janet Blair.

Q. The World War II television drama series "Garrison's Gorillas" starred what Turtle Creek native as Lt. Craig Garrison?

A. Ron Harper.

Q. What Philadelphia-born TV star hosts *America's Funniest Home Videos*?

A. Bob Saget.

Q. The group Cyrkle, formed in Easton in 1962, attained a gold record for what 1966 single?

A. "Red Rubber Ball."

Q. Philadelphia-born producer Herman Levin received a 1957 Tony Award for what Broadway production?

A. *My Fair Lady.*

Q. Pittsburgh-born actor and singer John Davidson co-hosted what television series with Cathy Lee Crosby and Fran Tarkenton?

A. *That's Incredible.*

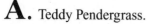

Q. What was the name of the famous Les Brown band?

A. Band of Renown.

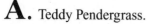

Q. Philadelphia native Andrea McArdle left the cast of *Search for Tomorrow* to star in what musical?

A. *Annie.*

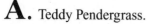

Q. What Pittsburgh-produced television show has been public television's longest-running children's program?

A. *Mister Rogers' Neighborhood.*

Q. Although confined to a wheelchair after an automobile accident, what Philadelphia-born singer continues to perform?

A. Teddy Pendergrass.

Q. The O'Jays reached number four in the charts with what 1978 single?

A. "Used to Be My Girl."

Q. What Pittsburgh-born talk show host and comedian got his start on *Saturday Night Live*?

A. Dennis Miller.

Q. On what television series did Philadelphia native Sherman Hemsley first become a regular?

A. *All in the Family,* as the Bunkers' neighbor George Jefferson.

———◆———

Q. An eight-foot bronze statue of what internationally known singer stands outside the Spectrum in Philadelphia?

A. Kate Smith.

———◆———

Q. What Pittsburgh native starred in the Philadelphia-filmed motion picture *Clean and Sober?*

A. Michael Keaton.

———◆———

Q. Freddy Cannon's popular hit "Palisades Park" was written by what Philadelphian?

A. Chuck Barris.

———◆———

Q. What western Pennsylvanian was the first moving picture director to use modern film know-how to tell a story?

A. Edwin S. Porter.

———◆———

Q. *Urban Cowboy* was a popular movie starring what Pittsburgh-born actor?

A. Scott Glenn.

———◆———

Q. For what film did Philadelphia-born writer/director Richard Brooks receive an Oscar in 1960?

A. *Elmer Gantry.*

Q. What Philadelphia-born actor starred with Julia Roberts in the movie *Pretty Woman*?

A. Richard Gere.

———◆———

Q. *Studio One,* the 1948–58 dramatic anthology series, paired what Brownsville-born actress with Charlton Heston in *The Taming of the Shrew*?

A. Lisa Kirk.

———◆———

Q. Philadelphia-native Ray Benson (born Seifert) was founder of what musical group that won a 1988 Grammy Award?

A. Asleep at the Wheel.

———◆———

Q. In what 1971 crime melodrama did Pittsburgh native Rita Gam appear with stars Jane Fonda and Donald Sutherland?

A. *KLUTE.*

———◆———

Q. Detective Joe Styles was portrayed by what Philadelphia-born actor on television's *Police Woman*?

A. Ed Bernard.

———◆———

Q. What prolific Pennsylvania movie producer created his first film, *Night of the Living Dead,* with friends from Carnegie Mellon University?

A. George Romero.

———◆———

Q. What actress from Philadelphia received an Academy Award for Best Actress during 1927–28 for three movies: *Seventh Heaven, Street Angel,* and *Sunrise*?

A. Janet Gaynor.

Q. Pen Argyl native Aldo Ray portrayed Sergeant Muldoon in what 1968 John Wayne war drama?

A. *The Green Berets.*

———◆———

Q. Philadelphian Norman Fell appeared as Detective Sergeant Charles Wilentz on what early 1970s crime show?

A. *Dan August.*

———◆———

Q. Phil Terry, Robert Edwards, Samuel Brown, and Eugene Daughtry formed what Philadelphia-based rhythm and blues vocal group?

A. The Intruders.

———◆———

Q. The TV show *The Fresh Prince of Bel Air* features what Philadelphia-born rapper?

A. Will Smith.

———◆———

Q. Las Vegas performer Lola Falana was born in what city?

A. Philadelphia.

———◆———

Q. Filmed in Pittsburgh, what 1987 movie told the story of a brain-damaged youth who worked as a garbage collector to send his intelligent brother through medical school?

A. *Dominick and Eugene.*

———◆———

Q. The 1950s Dean Martin hit "You're Nobody Till Somebody Loves You" was written by what Scranton native?

A. Russ Morgan.

Q. Philadelphia's Lionel, Ethel, and John Barrymore appeared together in what 1932 motion picture?

A. *Rasputin and the Empress.*

Q. Since 1955 what pop hit by Bill Haley and the Comets has sold more than 22.5 million copies?

A. "Rock around the Clock."

Q. What Philadelphia-born TV sportscaster was the host of *ABC's Wide World of Sports* from its premiere in 1961?

A. Jim McKay.

Q. What singer born and raised in Titusville became a partner with country vocalist Jack Greene in 1969?

A. Jeannie Seely.

Q. Hal Holbrook, Adrienne Barbeau, and E. G. Marshall starred in what 1982 horror film shot in Pittsburgh?

A. *Creepshow.*

Q. Frank Hardy of *The Hardy Boys* mystery series was played by what Philadelphia-born actor?

A. Parker Stevenson.

Q. What Pittsburgh-born Big Band singer launched his career with the songs "Jelly, Jelly" and "Stormy Monday Blues"?

A. Billy Eckstine.

Q. Pittsburgh native Bill Cullen was a regular panelist on what prime time game show that ran from 1952 to 1967?

A. *I've Got a Secret.*

Q. In February 1962 what Philadelphia-born singer produced her first hit single, "Mashed Potato Time"?

A. Dee Dee Sharp.

Q. Pennsylvania native James Stewart starred as a patriotic young senator in what 1939 film?

A. *Mr. Smith Goes to Washington.*

Q. Philadelphia-born actress Melanie Mayron portrayed Terry Simon in what film starring Jack Lemmon and Sissy Spacek?

A. *Missing.*

Q. Pittsburgh native Frank Gorshin portrayed what character on the television series *Batman*?

A. The Riddler.

Q. What is the last name of the Philadelphia-born 1950s teen idol, Fabian?

A. Forte.

Q. Tommy Dorsey, the famous bandleader of the swing era, was a master of what instrument?

A. Trombone.

Q. In 1979 what Philadelphian joined with Rolling Stones' guitarists Ron Wood and Keith Richards to tour as the New Barbarians?

A. Stanley Clarke.

Q. Myron Fowler, owner of the competitive Peerless Detective Agency, was portrayed by what Philadelphian on television's *Simon & Simon,* 1981–83?

A. Eddie Barth.

Q. What 1987 psychological thriller was filmed in Pittsburgh?

A. *Monkey Shines.*

Q. What was the original name of Philadelphia-born actor W. C. Fields?

A. William Claude Dukenfield.

Q. Freeport native Don Taylor portrayed young police officer Jimmy Halloran in what 1948 crime story?

A. *The Naked City.*

Q. What Philadelphia-born actor starred in the film *Footloose?*

A. Kevin Bacon.

Q. Filmed in Philadelphia, what 1987 production starred Mark Harmon as a former Phillies player?

A. *Stealing Home.*

Q. Philadelphia-born writer N. Richard Nash created what play that later was made into a movie by the same name starring Burt Lancaster and Katharine Hepburn?

A. *The Rainmaker.*

◆

Q. Where in 1896 was the first motion picture shown to the general public in Pennsylvania?

A. Keith's Bijou Theater, Philadelphia.

◆

Q. Connellsville-born actor Justin Deas played what character in the original cast of TV's *Ryan's Hope*?

A. Dr. Bucky Carter.

◆

Q. Born in Pittsburgh on March 22, 1943, what singer/guitarist is known for such hit singles as "This Masquerade" and "Give Me the Night"?

A. George Benson.

◆

Q. Monongahela-born Roland Kibbee received an Emmy Award in 1982 as executive producer for what situation comedy?

A. *Barney Miller.*

◆

Q. What Philadelphia-born actress appeared in the films *The Three Musketeers, Pal Joey,* and *A Connecticut Yankee*?

A. Vivienne Segal.

◆

Q. Philadelphian Chuck Barris began hosting what TV game show on June 14, 1976?

A. *The Gong Show.*

HISTORY

Q. Made for President Washington from his own silverware, what were the first coins produced at the U.S. Mint in Philadelphia?

A. Half-dimes.

◆

Q. In 1869 what was the first product bottled by Henry J. Heinz in the basement of his Sharpsburg home?

A. Horseradish.

◆

Q. Lifting off from the courtyard of the Walnut Street Prison in Philadelphia, who made the nation's first balloon flight on January 9, 1793?

A. Jean-Pierre Blanchard.

◆

Q. The Skew Arch railroad bridge erected in Reading in 1857 was given what nickname because of the material its model was made from and the type of salary paid some workers?

A. "Soap and whiskey bridge."

◆

Q. In 1910 what famous evangelist held a crusade in New Castle, recording more than six thousand converts?

A. Billy Sunday.

Q. What Indian leader is remembered for the "Blood Rock incident" where she bashed in the skulls of several captive settlers following the Battle of Wyoming in 1778?

A. Queen Esther ("white queen" of the Seneca).

Q. In 1933 at State College High School, Professor Amos Neyhart of Penn State became the first in the nation to teach what class?

A. Driver Education.

Q. In the 1700s long rifles manufactured in the Lancaster area received what erroneous title?

A. Kentucky rifles.

Q. What hat manufacturer established his factory in Philadelphia in 1865 and became the largest maker of hats in America?

A. John Stetson.

Q. What U.S. president donated a pipe organ to the St. Paul's Presbyterian Church in Somerset?

A. William McKinley.

Q. What lighthouse was the first constructed on the Great Lakes in 1813?

A. The Land Lighthouse.

Q. What governmental body met at York from September 30, 1777, to June 27, 1778?

A. The Continental Congress.

Q. What aviation pioneer launched his first rubber-band-powered model flying machine from the Allegheny Observatory of Pittsburgh in 1891?

A. Samuel P. Langley.

───◆───

Q. Who first publicly read the Declaration of Independence to the townspeople of Philadelphia?

A. Capt. John Nixon.

───◆───

Q. Under what name in 1828 did the world's first labor party organize in Pennsylvania?

A. The Workingmen's Party.

───◆───

Q. How many Pennsylvanians were unemployed in 1931 during the Great Depression?

A. Almost 900,000.

───◆───

Q. What Uniontown-born soldier and statesman received the 1953 Nobel Peace Prize?

A. Gen. George Catlett Marshall.

───◆───

Q. Constructed in 1823, what is the oldest canal tunnel in America?

A. The Lebanon Canal Tunnel.

───◆───

Q. What building, erected in Homesdale in 1842, became one of the first structures of its type in the nation to be constructed of concrete?

A. The Allen Hotel.

Q. What "grey-eyed man of destiny" received a degree from the University of Pennsylvania Medical College in 1843 and later became president of Nicaragua?

A. William Walker.

Q. What automobile manufacturer graduated from Lehigh University in 1884?

A. James Ward Packard.

Q. What institution was founded in 1949 to provide historical information about the United States and to foster appreciation of the nation's political, social, and economic systems?

A. Freedoms Foundation at Valley Forge.

Q. What pioneer radio station started broadcasting from Grove City College in 1920?

A. WSAJ.

Q. How many National Guardsmen were sent to restore order during the steel strike at Homestead in 1892?

A. Eight thousand.

Q. What did the Delaware Indians call themselves?

A. *Leni-Lenape* (real men).

Q. Who was known as "the white woman of the Genesee"?

A. Mary Jemison.

Q. Featuring free love and worship services in the nude, what religious sect was founded in Montgomery County during the mid-1800s by Theophilus Gates?

A. The Battle Axes.

———◆———

Q. What German immigrant and one-time Pennsylvania resident invented steel wire cable and designed the Brooklyn Bridge?

A. John A. Roebling.

———◆———

Q. In what year did the Republican Party, Democratic Party, and the National Progressive Party all select Philadelphia as their national convention site?

A. 1948 (nominating Thomas E. Dewey, Harry S. Truman, and Henry A. Wallace, respectively).

———◆———

Q. What kind of disaster wiped out most of Carbondale on December 15, 1850?

A. Fire.

———◆———

Q. Built in 1700, what is thought to be Pennsylvania's oldest church?

A. Gloria Dei (Old Swedes'), Philadelphia.

———◆———

Q. What traffic flow rule observed daily by millions of Americans originated in Pennsylvania?

A. Driving on the right.

———◆———

Q. How many dollars' worth of Liberty and Victory bonds were purchased by Pennsylvanians during the First World War?

A. $2,709,947,800.

Q. What version of the submarine sandwich received its name from being a lunchtime favorite of workers in a Philadelphia shipyard?

A. "Hoggies," later changed to "hoagies" (Hog Island Shipyard).

Q. Under the election law of 1799, what item was introduced into Pennsylvania voting?

A. The printed ballot.

Q. What Pennsylvania community maintains the largest historic district outside of Philadelphia?

A. York.

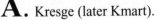

Q. What communication system was completed between Harrisburg and Lancaster in 1846?

A. Telegraph.

Q. In 1959 Harry B. Cunningham, a one-time Harrisburg newspaper reporter, revolutionized retail marketing when he became president of what department store chain?

A. Kresge (later Kmart).

Q. The inscription on the Liberty Bell comes from what biblical source?

A. Leviticus 25:10.

Q. What was the estimated total of both Union and Confederate dead and wounded from the Battle of Gettysburg, July 1–3, 1863?

A. Approximately 51,000.

Q. Who in 1935 became the first Democrat to hold the office of governor in Pennsylvania in almost fifty years?

A. George Howard Earle.

———◆———

Q. On the afternoon of July 3, 1863, how many cannon balls were fired during the monumental artillery duels at the Battle of Gettysburg?

A. More than 31,000.

———◆———

Q. The SS *Manhattan,* converted to an icebreaker by the Pennsylvania firm Sun Shipbuilding & Crydock Company, made what historic voyage in 1969?

A. The Northwest Passage.

———◆———

Q. In what year was the first Philadelphia-Pittsburgh Turnpike completed?

A. 1818.

———◆———

Q. What Philadelphia institution traces the history of black culture in the Americas?

A. Afro-American Historical and Cultural Museum.

———◆———

Q. What nickname was given to the aborted South Penn Railroad construction project that cost some 2,300 lives and $10 million between 1883 and 1885?

A. "Vanderbilt's Folly."

———◆———

Q. Around 1797, Pennsylvanian William P. Eichbaum became the first person to construct what type of lighting fixture in America?

A. A crystal chandelier.

Q. Who in 1819 received a charter from the Pennsylvania legislature to construct the first railroad in the Commonwealth?

A. Henry Drinker.

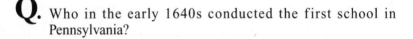

Q. Approximately how many lives were lost in the disastrous Johnstown flood of 1889?

A. 2,200.

Q. Who in the early 1640s conducted the first school in Pennsylvania?

A. Christopher Taylor.

Q. When was Pennsylvania's first Jewish synagogue dedicated?

A. 1782 (in Philadelphia).

Q. Whom did the Anti-Masonic Party succeed in electing as governor of Pennsylvania in 1835?

A. Joseph Ritner.

Q. What Philadelphian was the second black cabinet member in U.S. history?

A. William Thaddeus Coleman Jr., appointed secretary of transportation by President Gerald Ford.

Q. Who founded the Pennsylvania Academy in 1749?

A. Benjamin Franklin.

Q. The first meeting of the Pennsylvania assembly was held in 1682 in what town?

A. Chester.

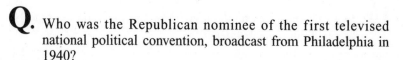

Q. Who was the Republican nominee of the first televised national political convention, broadcast from Philadelphia in 1940?

A. Wendell Willkie.

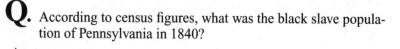

Q. According to census figures, what was the black slave population of Pennsylvania in 1840?

A. Sixty-four.

Q. What Beaver resident controlled the powerful Pennsylvania Republican machine during the late 1800s?

A. Matthew S. Quay.

Q. The Bedford area was the haunt of what self-styled Robin Hood in the early 1800s?

A. Davy Lewis.

Q. What mass transit system was built in Philadelphia in 1880?

A. Elevated railroad.

Q. What percentage of the school-aged children in Pennsylvania actually attended school in 1831?

A. Approximately 37 percent.

Q. What anarchist shot and stabbed industrialist Henry Clay Frick in an 1892 assassination attempt?

A. Alexander Berkman.

◆

Q. In 1792 what became the first public building and land owned by the federal government?

A. The U.S. Mint at 7th and Arch Streets, Philadelphia.

◆

Q. What Massachusetts automobile manufacturing pioneer moved his operations to Reading in 1900?

A. Charles E. Duryea.

◆

Q. In 1912 what college for Polish-American youths opened at Cambridge Springs?

A. Alliance College.

◆

Q. How many muskets were picked up on the field following the Battle of Gettysburg?

A. More than 27,000.

◆

Q. On July 4, 1876, what feminist leader read her famous "Declaration of Rights for Women" in front of Independence Hall?

A. Susan B. Anthony.

◆

Q. How many brothers comprised "the fighting Butlers" from Carlisle who all received commissions for bravery during the Revolutionary War?

A. Five.

Q. As a result of the Spanish-American War, what Pottsville native served as the military governor in both Cuba and Puerto Rico?

A. Maj. Gen. John R. Brooks.

Q. What world-famous stone railroad bridge was constructed at Lanesboro in 1847–48?

A. The Starrucca Viaduct.

Q. At what Philadelphia auditorium was President Ulysses S. Grant nominated for his second term?

A. The Academy of Music.

Q. The manufacture of what type of products brought Eddystone to national importance during World War I?

A. Munitions.

Q. One of the many smaller religious sects seeking religious freedom in Pennsylvania was the German Baptist Brethren, who were known by what nickname?

A. Dunkers.

Q. What Philadelphian served as vice president under President James K. Polk?

A. George Mifflin Dallas.

Q. Established in 1879, what was the first nonreservation school for Indians in the nation?

A. Carlisle Indian School, at Carlisle Barracks, now the site of the U.S. Army War College.

Q. To what longtime friend did Benjamin Franklin give the construction plans for, and all profits from, the stove that came to bear his name?

A. Robert Grave.

Q. What Pittsburgh printer's helper assisted Joseph Smith in the founding of Mormonism?

A. Sidney Rigdon.

Q. In what year did the Federal Constitutional Convention meet in Philadelphia?

A. 1787.

Q. What Scranton firm became the nation's first recipient of a federal common carrier license on December 22, 1936?

A. Rodger's Motor Lines.

Q. Whose likeness appeared on the nation's first five-cent stamp in 1847?

A. Benjamin Franklin.

Q. At its new Broad Street Station in 1884, the Pennsylvania Railroad established what "first" to transport passengers to center-city hotels?

A. Taxi service (The Hansom Cab).

Q. What was Betsy Ross's full name?

A. Elizabeth Griscom Ross.

Q. Why was the Liberty Bell carefully tapped several times in 1959?

A. To record its sound.

Q. Upon being appointed the first chief of the U.S. Navy's Medical Bureau in 1842, Philadelphian Dr. William P. C. Barton banned what practice aboard warships?

A. Drinking alcohol.

Q. Who founded Lehigh University at Bethlehem in 1866?

A. Asa Packer.

Q. The Historical Society in Philadelphia houses what gift given to William Penn as a token of peace by Indian friends?

A. A wampum belt.

Q. What Speaker of the U.S. House of Representatives was born in Harrisburg June 17, 1943?

A. Newt Gingrich.

Q. What type of floor covering was introduced in Lancaster in 1925?

A. Embossed inlaid linoleum.

Q. What was Andrew Carnegie's weekly income as a bobbin boy in a Pittsburgh cotton mill?

A. $1.20.

Q. The folding machine was patented by what Kennett Square resident in 1856?

A. Cyrus Chambers.

Q. Although the Liberty Bell had to be recast in Philadelphia in 1753, what firm originally produced it in 1751?

A. Whitechapel Foundry of London.

Q. In 1776 where did Philadelphia rank internationally in size of English-speaking cities?

A. Second only to London.

Q. What was the cost of the Pennsylvania canal system constructed during the 1820s and 1830s?

A. More than $33 million.

Q. Who made the world's first public radio address in 1921 from the Duquesne Club in Pittsburgh?

A. Herbert Hoover.

Q. How many Pennsylvanians signed the Declaration of Independence?

A. Nine.

Q. Constructed in 1677, what was the first major road in Pennsylvania?

A. King's Path (later called King's Highway).

Q. A Carlisle bank on December 1, 1909, inaugurated what seasonal savings plan that has become popular nationwide?

A. Christmas Club.

Q. In 1643 for what monarch did Johan Printz establish the first permanent colonial settlement in Pennsylvania country?

A. Queen Christina of Sweden.

Q. Cold War jitters led to the 1959 exhibition in Pleasant Hills of the nation's first home featuring what built-in facility?

A. A nuclear bomb shelter.

Q. How many days did it rain during the 187 operational days of the 1926 Philadelphia World's Fair?

A. 127.

Q. What religious sect organized its first church at Brush Run on May 4, 1811?

A. The Disciples of Christ (First Church of the Christian Association).

Q. The Todd House at 4th and Walnut Streets in Philadelphia was the home of what famous American?

A. Dolley Payne Todd (later wife of President James Madison).

Q. Chain smoking Conestoga wagoneers created what tobacco product term?

A. "Stogie" cigars.

Q. Pennsylvania distributed free "donation lands" to veterans of what war?

A. Revolutionary War.

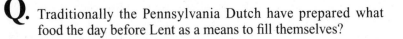

Q. What fundraising activity of the Girl Scouts had its beginning in Philadelphia in 1933?

A. The Girl Scout cookie sale.

Q. In 1965 what education facility became the first community college chartered in the western region of the Commonwealth?

A. Butler County Community College.

Q. Constructed at Brownsville in 1813, what was the first steamboat to ply the waters of the Monogahela, Ohio, and Mississippi Rivers?

A. The *Comet.*

Q. Traditionally the Pennsylvania Dutch have prepared what food the day before Lent as a means to fill themselves?

A. *Fassnachts* (deep-fried doughnuts).

Q. Philadelphian Frederic Eugene Ives revolutionized the printing and publishing industries with which two processes?

A. Halftones (1878) and three-color process printing (1886).

Q. What Blue Bell resident set a women's world ballooning record on January 9, 1976, by reaching an altitude of 14,000 feet and covering a distance of 400 miles?

A. Constance Wolf.

Q. On October 4, 1906, what individual dedicated the state capitol?

A. President Theodore Roosevelt.

Q. In December 1790 who became the first governor of the commonwealth of Pennsylvania?

A. Thomas Mifflin.

Q. What white pioneer, born in 1741 near present-day Harrisburg, led Indians in many raids against colonists?

A. Simon Girty.

Q. What Bedford home served as the headquarters of President George Washington during the Whiskey Rebellion in 1794?

A. The Espy House.

Q. By 1776 where did Pennsylvania rank in population among the English colonies in North America?

A. Third.

Q. Philadelphian Elaine Peden successfully attained what goal when President Ronald Reagan signed a proclamation in 1984?

A. American citizenship for William and Hannah Penn.

Q. What Johnstown company in 1855 became the first in the nation to produce thirty-foot rolled steel rails?

A. Cambria Iron Works.

Q. Who was the founder and president of both the U.S. Steel Corporation and the Bethlehem Steel Corporation?

A. Charles M. Schwab.

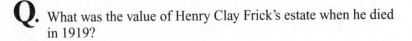

Q. What was the value of Henry Clay Frick's estate when he died in 1919?

A. $120 million.

Q. Who deprived William Penn of governing authority over Pennsylvania from October 1692 until August 1694?

A. William and Mary, joint sovereigns of England.

Q. What businessman and philanthropist bequeathed his estate to establish a school for male orphans in Philadelphia?

A. Stephen Girard (Girard College).

Q. What pictures appear on the U.S. one hundred-dollar bill?

A. Benjamin Franklin and Independence Hall.

Q. Where in 1742 was America's first girls' school established?

A. Germantown.

Q. What Philadelphian in 1807 established the first looms in Pennsylvania for the manufacturing of oilcloth and floor coverings?

A. John Dorsey.

Q. In the only trial of its kind in Pennsylvania, Margaret Mattson was tried on what charges in February 1683?

A. Witchcraft.

Q. What Pennsylvania regiment was the first to respond to President Lincoln's war proclamation?

A. Ringgold Light Artillery, Reading.

Q. The pews of Benjamin Franklin and George Washington may be seen in what Pennsylvania church?

A. Christ Church, Second Street in Philadelphia.

Q. What Gladwyne native was commander of the Army Air Corps during World War II?

A. Gen. Henry H. Arnold.

Q. Where did George Washington and his Continental soldiers bivouac during the winter of 1777–78?

A. Valley Forge.

Q. What nostalgic term refers to the covered bridges of Pennsylvania?

A. "Kissin' bridges."

Q. The Big Mill in Reading, now housing outlet shopping, at one time was a shoe factory producing what type of special shoes for young ladies?

A. Official Girl Scout shoes.

Q. The Airmail Act was introduced by what Pennsylvania congressman in 1925?

A. Clyde Kelly.

Q. What unusually designed house was built at New Castle by Frank Phillis around 1863?

A. The Ten-Sided House (an imperfect decagon).

Q. In 1934 what secretary of the United Mine Workers of America was elected lieutenant governor of Pennsylvania?

A. Thomas Kennedy.

Q. Stemming from a movement started by Quakers in 1688, Pennsylvania on February 29, 1780, became the first state to pass what type of law?

A. Abolition.

Q. What rail line inaugurated horsecar service in Philadelphia in 1855?

A. North Penn Railway.

Q. What religious sect under the leadership of George Rapp established a collectivist community at Harmony in 1803 and later at Ambridge?

A. The Harmony Society, or Harmonites.

Q. What federal financial institution was opened in Philadelphia in 1791?

A. The Bank of the United States.

Q. What law with regard to education was passed by the Pennsylvania legislature in 1895?

A. Compulsory school attendance.

Q. In 1791 what group of craftsmen conducted the nation's first labor strike?

A. Philadelphia carpenters.

Q. In 1771 the Pennsylvania assembly declared what natural feature as public highways?

A. Rivers.

Q. What future president studied medicine for several months at the University of Pennsylvania?

A. William Henry Harrison.

Q. In 1844 what led to the call up of the militia to restore order in Philadelphia?

A. Anti-Catholic riots.

Q. What piece of heavy equipment with the nickname "Amphibian Monster" was constructed by Oliver Evans in 1804?

A. A steam dredge.

Q. In 1895 what judicial division was established in the Commonwealth to help relieve the State's supreme court caseload?

A. The Superior Court.

Q. To whom did Peter Armstrong deed land holdings of the Celestial Community of Adventists near Laporte when the commune disbanded in 1864?

A. "Almighty God."

---◆---

Q. What was the fare for passengers on the Pennsylvania Canal in the early 1830s?

A. Two cents per mile.

---◆---

Q. What document drawn up by William Penn and endorsed by the assembly in 1701 became the basic core of Pennsylvania law until 1776?

A. Charter of Privileges.

---◆---

Q. When the Pennsylvania Turnpike first opened in 1940, what was the fixed speed limit?

A. None.

---◆---

Q. Who was the principal speaker when the Gettysburg National Cemetery was dedicated?

A. The well-known orator Edward Everett.

---◆---

Q. By 1706 what road connected Philadelphia with Chester?

A. The Queen's Road.

---◆---

Q. In 1609, what British explorer sailed into Delaware Bay looking for a trade route to the Far East?

A. Henry Hudson.

Q. What 1923 legislative bill closed down state licensed saloons for the duration of the Prohibition era?

A. The Snyder Act.

———◆———

Q. Completed in 1953, what Pittsburgh structure became the world's first aluminum-faced building?

A. Alcoa Building.

———◆———

Q. Philadelphia John P. Carlton copyrighted what postal product in 1861?

A. The postcard.

———◆———

Q. Rev. John Winebrenner of Harrisburg split from the German Reformed Church to establish what religious group?

A. The Church of God of North America.

———◆———

Q. What president maintained a house and farm at Gettysburg?

A. Dwight D. Eisenhower.

———◆———

Q. In 1852 New Wilmington became the home of what co-educational institution?

A. Westminster College.

———◆———

Q. The opening of what seaway in 1959 gave Erie water access to the ports of the world?

A. The Saint Lawrence Seaway.

Q. In September 1941 what uniquely styled building (made internationally famous by the military) was first constructed at Greenwich?

A. Quonset hut.

Q. What did squatters who settled west of Lycoming Creek during the 1700s call themselves?

A. Fair Play Men.

Q. Launched at Pittsburgh in 1811, what was the name of the first steamboat to ply the waters of the Ohio and Mississippi Rivers?

A. The *New Orleans*.

Q. Built in 1816, the Bedford Springs Hotel served as a summer White House for which U.S. president?

A. James Buchanan.

Q. During what 1794 uprising did President George Washington send 12,950 troops into western Pennsylvania to help restore order?

A. Whiskey Insurrection.

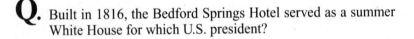

Q. Out of what Philadelphia church was the first presbytery in America formed?

A. Buttonwood Presbyterian Church.

Q. In 1829 what Pennsylvania firm became the first in the nation to use an imported steam locomotive?

A. The Delaware and Hudson Canal Company.

Q. What wagon design that proved to be a popular mode of pioneer transportation originated in Lancaster County?

A. The Conestoga wagon.

———◆———

Q. Who is known as "the father of the plate glass industry in America"?

A. Capt. John B. Ford.

———◆———

Q. What Pennsylvania institution of higher education became the first in the nation to employ an all-black faculty?

A. Allegheny Institute, later called Avery College.

———◆———

Q. Although the legend that Betsy Ross made the first flag that had stars and stripes is probably untrue, what was her known role in flagmaking?

A. She was an official flagmaker for the Pennsylvania Navy.

———◆———

Q. What notorious Revolutionary War general was born near the present-day community of Wayne in 1745?

A. Gen. "Mad Anthony" Wayne.

———◆———

Q. Who in 1882 became Pennsylvania's first Democratic governor to be elected after the Civil War?

A. Robert Emory Pattison.

———◆———

Q. Formed in Pennsylvania in 1724, what was the name of the nation's first craft association?

A. The Carpenters' Company.

Q. Who concocted the first ice cream soda in Philadelphia in 1874?

A. Robert M. Green.

———◆———

Q. On June 1, 1887, Bethlehem Iron Company became the first firm in America to receive a contract from the U.S. Navy for the manufacture of what product?

A. Armor plate.

———◆———

Q. Under what name was Duquesne University founded in 1878?

A. The College of the Holy Ghost.

———◆———

Q. During World War I, how many Pennsylvanians served in the military?

A. 370,961.

———◆———

Q. Who erected America's first paper mill in Pennsylvania in 1690?

A. William Rittenhouse.

———◆———

Q. In 1832 what became the first institution of higher learning to be established at Collegeville?

A. Todd's School.

———◆———

Q. At the Battle of Bushy Run in 1763, Col. Henry Bouquet utilized what type of supplies to construct a barricade to shelter his wounded men?

A. Bags of flour.

Q. Where did M. S. Hershey manufacture caramel prior to the establishment of his planned community of Hershey?

A. Lancaster.

———◆———

Q. Arriving in 1808 from New York, what was the name of the first steamship to dock at Philadelphia?

A. The *Phoenix*.

———◆———

Q. In 1776–77, what delegate from Pennsylvania was the chief author of the first draft of the Articles of Confederation?

A. John Dickinson.

———◆———

Q. The 1798 Fries Rebellion, mounted by Pennsylvanians in resistance to national taxation, was known by what other title?

A. Hot-Water Rebellion.

———◆———

Q. What noted colonial evangelist was instrumental in the relocation of Moravians from Georgia to Pennsylvania in 1740?

A. George Whitefield.

———◆———

Q. In 1831 Matthias Baldwin introduced what industry to Pennsylvania?

A. Locomotive and railroad car construction.

———◆———

Q. What name was given to the Pennsylvania detachment that on April 18, 1861, was rushed to Washington to stay an impending Confederate attack?

A. First Defenders.

Q. What was the construction cost of the Pennsylvania Turnpike?

A. $70 million.

Q. Who was the guest of honor at the opening of the Philadelphia Centennial Exhibition in April 1876?

A. Ulysses S. Grant.

Q. What Carlisle resident was the heroine of the Battle of Monmouth in 1778?

A. Molly Pitcher.

Q. In 1765 what famous inventor was born between the present-day communities of Mechanics Grove and Wakefield in Lancaster County?

A. Robert Fulton.

Q. Prior to the advent of the steamboat, what type of boats measuring sixty feet in length and eight feet in width were the primary freight haulers on the Delaware River and its tributaries?

A. Durham boats.

Q. What eighteenth-century German immigrant became Pennsylvania's foremost Indian treatymaker?

A. Conrad Weiser.

Q. Who in 1746 constructed Pennsylvania's first nail factory at Glen Mills?

A. John Taylor.

Q. During the Civil War, a letter from Rev. N. R. Watkinson of Ridleyville to the secretary of the treasury, Salmon P. Chase, set in motion the eventual development of what motto?

A. In God We Trust.

———◆———

Q. Who served as White House hostess for the nation's only bachelor president?

A. Harriet Lane, niece and ward of James Buchanan.

———◆———

Q. By what name was the University of Pittsburgh called on its original charter?

A. Pittsburgh Academy.

———◆———

Q. On what two ships did Johan Printz and his party arrive at Tinicum Island in February 1643 to establish Fort Gottenburg?

A. *Fama* and *Svanen*.

———◆———

Q. Where did Pennsylvania rank among Union states in the number of men supplied during the Civil War?

A. Second only to New York.

———◆———

Q. What early Pennsylvania church leader is known as "the patriarch of the Lutheran Church in America"?

A. Dr. Henrich Melchoir Muhlenberg.

———◆———

Q. What legislation was passed in Pennsylvania in 1903 to help protect school teachers' income?

A. Minimum salary law.

Q. What sect split from mainline Pennsylvania Quakers in order to bear arms during the Revolutionary War?

A. Free Quakers.

Q. Into what college did Farmers' High School in Centre County evolve?

A. Pennsylvania State College.

Q. In 1786 Pennsylvania printers advocated what minimum wage for their trade?

A. Six dollars per week.

Q. In 1906 what mode of transportation was developed to link Clarks Summit with Scranton?

A. An electric railway.

Q. Who first brought Methodism to Pennsylvania in 1768?

A. Capt. Thomas Webb.

Q. What was the average weight of a Conestoga wagon?

A. 3,000 to 3,500 pounds.

Q. Eighteenth-century German immigrant Baron Henry William Stiegel established what type of company near Manheim in Lancaster County?

A. Glass works.

Q. Who led Tories and Indians against settlers at the Battle of Wyoming in July 1778?

A. Maj. John Butler.

Q. In 1832 the Northumberland Baptist Association laid the groundwork for what Lewisburg institution of higher learning that opened in 1846?

A. Bucknell University (formerly the University of Lewisburg).

Q. What was the real name of "Molly Pitcher"?

A. Mary Ludwig Hays.

Q. In 1978, what foreign automobile maker opened its first U.S. assembly plant near New Stanton?

A. Volkswagenwerk AG.

Q. During the Civil War what name was given to the regiment of the Pennsylvania Reserve Corps comprised chiefly of volunteers from McKean, Elk, and Cameron Counties?

A. Bucktail Boys (Bucktail Regiment).

Q. According to the first federal census, what was the population of Pennsylvania in 1790?

A. 434,373.

Q. What type of industry brought Sheffield into existence in 1864?

A. Tanneries.

Q. What Philadelphian in 1804 established the nation's first successful printer's ink manufacturing firm?

A. Charles Eneu Johnson.

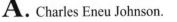

Q. By 1776 what portion of Pennsylvania's residents were of German origin?

A. About one third.

Q. What Lutheran minister founded Susquehanna University of Selinsgrove in 1858?

A. Rev. Benjamin Kurtz.

Q. What labor organization was formed in Pittsburgh in 1881?

A. Federation of Organized Trades and Labor Union (later AFL).

Q. Who constructed America's first practical tramroad track at Leiperville in 1809?

A. Thomas Leiper.

Q. America's first crushed stone road, the Philadelphia and Lancaster Pike completed in 1794, cost how much per mile to construct?

A. $7,500.

Q. What was the name of America's first frigate, launched at the Philadelphia shipyards in 1797?

A. *United States.*

Q. What unusual celibate community was established at Ephrata in Lancaster County under the direction of Conrad Beissel in the late 1700s?

A. Seventh-day Baptist.

Q. What was the first functioning institution of higher learning in America designated a university?

A. The University of Pennsylvania (1791).

Q. In gratitude for his help in bringing peace to the frontier, Pennsylvania voted a grant of land near present-day Warren to what Seneca Indian chief?

A. Cornplanter (1740–1836).

Q. What U.S. secretary of state was born in Scranton on October 10, 1925?

A. Warren Christopher (under President Bill Clinton).

Q. In what year did the present U.S. Mint facility in Philadelphia open?

A. 1969.

Q. What is the Pennsylvania state motto?

A. Virtue, Liberty, and Independence.

Q. What religious sect took advantage of Pennsylvania's religious freedom and settled in Germantown in 1682–83?

A. Mennonites.

Q. In 1913 what world's first service for motorists was opened in Pittsburgh?

A. A drive-in gas station.

◆

Q. What Pennsylvania lawyer and U.S. congressman who led the movement to impeach President Andrew Johnson championed public schools in the state legislature?

A. Thaddeus Stevens.

◆

Q. What gift was given by Italian citizens of Philadelphia to the city on the occasion of the U.S. Centennial Exposition in 1876?

A. Christopher Columbus Statue (now located at Marconi Plaza).

◆

Q. In what year was Harrisburg chosen as the state capital?

A. 1812.

◆

Q. In 1865 the Walnut Theatre in Philadelphia was bought and rebuilt by what gentlemen?

A. John S. Clarke and his brother-in-law, Edwin Booth (brother of John Wilkes Booth).

◆

Q. What was the first collegiate business school in the nation?

A. Wharton School, University of Pennsylvania.

◆

Q. Founded in Pittsburgh in 1807, what was the first successful flint glass factory in the nation?

A. Bakewell & Page.

ARTS & LITERATURE

Q. What 1875 Thomas Eakins painting has been called by many critics "America's greatest masterpiece"?

A. *The Gross Clinic.*

———◆———

Q. A story penned by Hanover attorney John Luther Long became what famous opera?

A. *Madame Butterfly.*

———◆———

Q. What musical instrument consisting of a row of rotating water-filled glass containers was invented by Benjamin Franklin?

A. The armonica.

———◆———

Q. In 1838 how many subscriptions to his first edition folio sets of *Birds of America* did John James Audubon sell in America and Europe at one thousand dollars each?

A. 161.

———◆———

Q. What short story written by Wyalusing native Phillip Van Doren Stern became the basis for the 1946 Frank Capra hit movie *It's a Wonderful Life*?

A. "The Greatest Gift: A Christmas Tale."

Q. In addition to being a jeweler's helper as a teenager in Philadelphia, how did Robert Fulton make a living?

A. Painting miniatures.

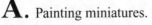

Q. Born in York, who became America's first native-born professional dancer?

A. John Durang.

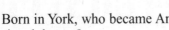

Q. The first public library outside of Philadelphia was in what community?

A. Darby.

Q. What theater, known for its excellent acoustics, is home to the Pittsburgh Symphony Orchestra?

A. Heinz Hall.

Q. What Springfield-born artist became the official painter of history to King George III in 1772?

A. Benjamin West.

Q. What great black tenor, called "the American Mario," was born in Philadelphia in 1836?

A. Thomas J. Bowers.

Q. During what years was the original Pittsburgh Orchestra in existence?

A. 1896–1910.

Q. Penn State defensive tackle Mike Reid received the 1986 Song of the Year award by the American Society of Composers, Authors, and Publishers for what composition?

A. "Lost in the Fifties."

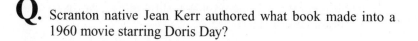

Q. "The Heart Turns Back" was one of several poems published by what Somerset County poet?

A. Marion Doyle.

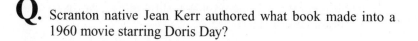

Q. Published in Philadelphia between 1828 and 1831, what was the name of the world's first labor journal?

A. *Mechanics' Free Press.*

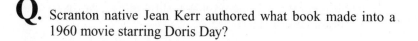

Q. Scranton native Jean Kerr authored what book made into a 1960 movie starring Doris Day?

A. *Please Don't Eat the Daisies.*

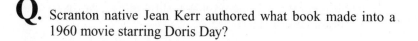

Q. What great nineteenth-century still-life painter once maintained a studio at 400 Locust Street in Philadelphia?

A. William Michael Harnett.

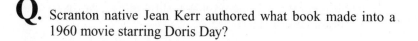

Q. In what year was Erie's first theater opened?

A. 1860.

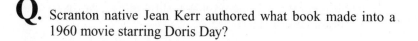

Q. What medieval-style Germanic stone house in Lancaster was depicted in several paintings by Andrew Wyeth?

A. Hans Herr House (Herr was Wyeth's ancestor).

Q. What Pennsylvania artist sculpted the groups of statuary at the front of the state capitol?

A. George Grey Barnard.

Q. More than four hundred exhibits of brass instruments are the focus of what rural Chester County museum?

A. The Trumpet Museum, Streitwieser Foundation.

Q. Fallingwater, a house dramatically stationed over a waterfall in Fayette County, was designed by what renowned architect in 1936?

A. Frank Lloyd Wright.

Q. What was the title of the nation's first magazine for the blind published by the Pennsylvania Institution for the Instruction of the Blind in January 1837?

A. *The Students Magazine.*

Q. How many paintings did Thomas Eakins sell during his lifetime?

A. Twenty.

Q. The Academy of Music in Philadelphia was modeled after what famous Italian auditorium?

A. Milan's famed La Scala.

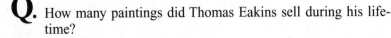

Q. What type of Pennsylvania pottery was made by coating basic redware with a thin coat of white clay, or "slip," then scratching a design that exposed the red clay?

A. Sgraffito.

Q. What name is given to various round signs incorporating stylized stars, rosettes, or wheels painted on Pennsylvania Dutch barns?

A. Hex signs (to ward off misfortune).

Q. Composed in 1840, what was Stephen Foster's first known work?

A. "Tioga Waltz."

Q. The world's largest collection of Andrew Wyeth paintings is displayed in what Delaware County museum?

A. The Brandywine River Museum.

Q. *Leonora,* America's first noteworthy opera, was composed by what Philadelphian in the mid-1840s?

A. William Fry.

Q. *Sea Garden,* published in 1916, was the first book by what noted Bethlehem-born poet?

A. Hilda Doolittle (H.D.).

Q. What author of western novels, including *Riders of the Purple Sage,* began his writing career in Lackawaxen?

A. Zane Grey.

Q. What is *fraktur,* examples of which are on display at the Ephrata Cloister?

A. A style of lettering used in German printing.

Q. What two South Carolina sisters relocated to Philadelphia and published antislavery and women's rights pamphlets in the 1830s?

A. Sarah Moore Grimké and Angelina Emily Grimké.

Q. Who designed the state capitol, which was completed in 1906?

A. Joseph M. Huston.

Q. What 1928 book brought international recognition to Pennsylvania-born anthropologist Margaret Mead?

A. *Coming of Age in Samoa.*

Q. What Norwegian violin virtuoso laid out such settlements as Oleona, New Bergen, and Walhalla during the mid-1800s in an attempt to create a "New Norway" in Pennsylvania?

A. Ole Borneman Bull.

Q. Philadelphia-born Joseph Kramm received a 1952 Pulitzer Prize for what dramatic play?

A. *The Shrike.*

Q. What black painter, born in Pittsburgh and trained at the Pennsylvania Academy of the Fine Arts, first gained recognition for his pictures of life on plantations?

A. Henry Ossawa Tanner.

Q. What is one of the nation's largest black newspapers, published in Pittsburgh?

A. *New Pittsburgh Courier.*

Q. McDonald-born composer Jay Livingston, along with Ray Evans, co-wrote what 1950 Christmas classic?

A. "Silver Bells."

Q. What female artist rendered many of the paintings in the state capitol?

A. Violet Oakley.

Q. What Wattsburg-born author brought muckraking journalism into vogue with her 1904 *History of the Standard Oil Company*?

A. Ida M. Tarbell.

Q. In 1731 what Philadelphian founded the first subscription library in the American colonies?

A. Benjamin Franklin.

Q. What repertory theater was established at Swarthmore in 1923 by Jasper Deeter?

A. Hedgerow Theater.

Q. "Deep River" was written by what Erie-born black composer?

A. Henry Thacker Burleigh.

Q. While he was living at Newtown, what was the primary occupation of folk artist Edward Hicks?

A. Sign painter.

Q. Where was the Ulman Opera House built around 1850?

A. Williamsport.

Q. What famous American sculptor created the work *Cowboy* in Philadelphia's Fairmount Park?

A. Frederic Remington.

Q. Who drew America's first editorial cartoon, which ran in the May 9, 1754, edition of the *Pennsylvania Gazette*?

A. Benjamin Franklin.

Q. What Scranton-born playwright married actress Helen Hayes in 1928?

A. Charles MacArthur.

Q. The eighteenth-century monastic community of Ephrata Cloister is depicted in what musical drama?

A. *Vorspiel.*

Q. What 1937 novel by Pine Grove native Conrad Richter was made into a motion picture?

A. *The Sea of Grass.*

Q. The Paoli studio and former home of what artist/craftsman features paintings, woodcuts, ceramics, furniture, and utensils?

A. Wharton Esherick.

Q. What vice president of the Curtis Publishing Company won the Pulitzer Prize in 1921 for his autobiography?

A. Edward Bok.

Q. What artist was known as "the poet and painter of the Susquehanna"?

A. Lloyd Mifflin.

Q. Abolitionist, woman suffragist, and noted reformer Jane Grey Swisshelm edited what Pittsburgh publication?

A. *Saturday Evening Visitor.*

Q. What is the third oldest metropolitan orchestra in the nation?

A. The Erie Philharmonic Orchestra.

Q. What type of tinware unique to Pennsylvania was decorated by an artist using a stylus to etch a pattern or punch a design?

A. Wiggleware.

Q. The statue of William Penn atop city hall in Philadelphia was created by what Philadelphia-born sculptor?

A. Alexander Milne Calder.

Q. What Philadelphian became the first black pianist in history to play a transcontinental tour?

A. Carl Rossini Diton.

Q. What famous children's publication had its beginning in York?

A. *My Weekly Reader.*

Q. Who built the nation's first permanent theater in Philadelphia in 1766?

A. David Douglass.

Q. Artist Alexander Calder became best known for creating what type of sculptures?

A. Mobiles.

Q. What was the first magazine published in the North American colonies, by Andrew Bradford of Philadelphia in 1741?

A. *The American Magazine or a Monthly View of the British Colonies* (it lasted three months).

Q. In 1930 what became the first successful work for Uniontown-born writer John Dickson Carr?

A. *It Walks by Night.*

Q. West Chester native Samuel Barber received the 1958 Pulitzer Prize for music for what opera?

A. *Vanessa.*

Q. What was Stephen Collins Foster's first published song?

A. "Open Thy Lattice, Love."

Q. David Brenner shares about his growing up in Philadelphia in what 1983 book?

A. *Soft Pretzels and Mustard.*

Q. With whom did Robert Fulton study painting in England?

A. Benjamin West.

Q. What Philadelphia-born director received a 1960 Tony Award for *The Miracle Worker*?

A. Arthur Penn.

Q. The Hungarian steel workers from the Allegheny County area created what bigger-than-life folk hero?

A. Joe Magarac (Hungarian for *jackass*).

Q. New Castle boasts what cultural complex situated on four acres of formal gardens and landscaped grounds?

A. The Hoyt Institute of Fine Arts.

Q. What essayist and lifetime Philadelphian was described by one critic as "the mistress of the finely tuned phrase"?

A. Agnes Repplier.

Q. What Pennsylvania painter wrote "Essay on Building Wooden Bridges" in 1797?

A. Charles Willson Peale.

Q. What 1966 best-selling novel did Jacqueline Susann write?

A. *Valley of the Dolls.*

Q. What artist, born in Lock Haven in 1871, was one of The Eight (called the Ashcan School by the critics)?

A. John Sloan.

Q. Because of its rich cultural life, Philadelphia received what title during colonial days?

A. "Athens of America."

Q. What great Pittsburgh-born playwright and director teamed with Morrie Ryskind in 1925 to create *The Cocoanuts* for the Marx Brothers?

A. George S. Kaufman.

Q. The Art Association of Harrisburg occupies what former Pennsylvania governor's home?

A. William Findlay.

Q. Harold V. Cohen of Wampum held what position at the *Pittsburgh Post-Gazette* for forty years?

A. Drama critic.

Q. *Appalachian Spring* was created by what dancer/choreographer who was born in a Pittsburgh suburb in 1894?

A. Martha Graham.

Q. What novel by Garet Garrett was set around Danville and its mills?

A. *The Cinder Buggy.*

◆

Q. The Southern Alleghenies Museum of Art is situated on what college campus?

A. St. Francis College, Loretto.

◆

Q. The musical play *Pal Joey* was written by what Pottsville-born author?

A. John O'Hara.

◆

Q. For what song did Pittsburgh-born lyricist Leo Robin win an Oscar in 1938?

A. "Thanks for the Memory."

◆

Q. What Philadelphia-born novelist became the nation's first full-time professional writer?

A. Charles Brockden Brown.

◆

Q. Singer/actress Ethel Waters wrote what 1951 autobiography?

A. *His Eye Is on the Sparrow.*

◆

Q. While living in Philadelphia during the 1790s, what portrait painter produced the most noted studies of George Washington?

A. Gilbert Stuart.

Q. What was the title of performer/producer Dick Clark's 1976 biography?

A. *Rock, Roll, and Remember.*

Q. What author often used the community of York as a backdrop for her novels, short stories, and poems?

A. Katherine Haviland-Taylor.

Q. Painter Charles Willson Peale fathered how many children?

A. Seventeen.

Q. What was America's first art museum?

A. Pennsylvania Academy of the Fine Arts.

Q. Where did eighteenth-century Philadelphia-born theatrical great Edwin Forrest Home make his first and last stage appearances?

A. Walnut Street Theater, Philadelphia.

Q. What Pennsylvanian composed the mining ballad "Down, Down, Down"?

A. William Keating.

Q. What noted editor of the *New York Tribune* was an employee of the Erie *Gazette* in 1830–31?

A. Horace Greeley.

Q. Lancaster's *Public Register and American Citizen* newspaper became known as a voice of what political party in 1853?

A. The Know-Nothing Party.

◆

Q. At what art museum are N.C. Wyeth's illustrations for *Treasure Island* displayed?

A. Brandywine River Museum, Chadds Ford.

◆

Q. The community of Atlantic was the birthplace of what playwright who wrote *Elizabeth the Queen* and *Winterset*?

A. Maxwell Anderson.

◆

Q. The Opera Company of Philadelphia sponsors what annual May contest?

A. The International Luciano Pavarotti Voice Competition.

◆

Q. *Appointment in Samarra, Hope of Heaven, Butterfield 8,* and *The Ewings* are just four of thirty-one books written by what Pottsville-born writer?

A. John O'Hara.

◆

Q. What Wilkes-Barre artist helped preserve a view of North America Indian culture through his paintings and illustrations?

A. George Catlin.

◆

Q. In 1932 Dublin resident Pearl S. Buck won the Pulitzer Prize for fiction for what novel?

A. *The Good Earth.*

Q. What Pittsburgh-born painter was known for her solid, weighty approach to impressionism?

A. Mary Cassatt.

Q. What musical organization was founded in 1893 by Dr. William Wallace Gilchrist to encourage Pennsylvania composers?

A. The Manuscript Music Society.

Q. Germantown founder Francis Daniel Pastorius compiled and published a vast encyclopedia of what title?

A. *Beehive.*

Q. In 1926 Pennsylvania-born playwright George Edward Kelly received a Pulitzer Prize for what work?

A. *Craig's Wife.*

Q. "Enjoy Yourself (It's Later Than You Think)" was a hit composition by what Braddock-born composer?

A. Herb Magidson.

Q. What Reading-born writer was called "the most finished poet of his age"?

A. Wallace Stevens.

Q. In Philadelphia on August 4, 1821, Samuel C. Atkinson and Charles Alexander inaugurated what popular periodical?

A. *Saturday Evening Post.*

Q. Founded in 1805, what Philadelphia institution is the oldest art school in the United States?

A. The Pennsylvania Academy of the Fine Arts.

———◆———

Q. In 1985, what staffer of the Philadelphia *Daily News* won a Pulitzer Prize for editorial writing?

A. Richard Aregood.

———◆———

Q. Published at the Philadelphia Latin School (William Penn Charter School) in 1777, what publication is said to have been the world's first student dissent "newspaper"?

A. *The Student Gazette.*

———◆———

Q. What book by J. W. Lippincott Jr. is credited with having brought to the attention of the nation the near-extinction of the whooping crane?

A. *Old Bill: The Whooping Crane.*

———◆———

Q. In the 1800s, what river town was immortalized in the popular lumberjack ballad "Camp Barber's Song"?

A. Port Allegany.

———◆———

Q. What Pennsylvania pioneer in American sculpture created the *Nymph of the Schuykill*?

A. William Rush.

———◆———

Q. What journalism award was won in 1787 by the *Pittsburgh Press* and in 1990 by the *Philadelphia Inquirer*?

A. Pulitzer Prize for meritorious public service.

Q. In 1904 Philadelphia artist Grace Gebbie Drayton created what new advertising gimmick for the magazine ads of Campbell Soup Company?

A. The Campbell Kid characters.

Q. What Potter County native became famous for his elaborate wood carvings?

A. John Scholl.

Q. In 1832 Elijah Worthington established what strongly opinionated publication at Wilkes-Barre?

A. *Anti-Masonic Advocate.*

Q. Who served as music director of the Philadelphia Orchestra from 1912 through 1941?

A. Leopold Stokowski.

Q. While in Philadelphia for the Centennial Exhibition, what poet visited St. David's Church and was inspired to pen "Old St. David's at Radnor"?

A. Henry Wadsworth Longfellow.

Q. What musical group performed the first documented recital in Pennsylvania in 1703?

A. The Hermits of the Wissahickon.

Q. What Philadelphia playhouse, built in 1808, is the oldest continuously used theater in the United States?

A. Walnut Street Theater.

Q. What Philadelphia-born author wrote the classic western novel *The Virginian*?

A. Owen Wister.

◆

Q. What English Quaker brought the first printing press to Pennsylvania in 1693?

A. William Bradford.

◆

Q. Philadelphia-raised painter Raphaelle patented what maritime product?

A. Preservative for ship timbers.

◆

Q. What Francis Biddle novel dealt with Philadelphia society?

A. *The Llanflar Pattern.*

◆

Q. What Philadelphia-born feature writer won the 1992 Pulitzer Prize for newspaper commentary?

A. Anna Quindlin (*New York Times*).

◆

Q. Who was the conductor of the all-black Philadelphia orchestra that performed for such personalities as General Lafayette and Queen Victoria?

A. Frank Johnson.

◆

Q. What Philadelphia building is the largest masonry-supported structure in the world?

A. City hall.

Q. What pop artist, born in Philadelphia, is remembered for his depictions of soup cans?

A. Andy Warhol.

Q. Revolutionary War figure Col. George Morgan penned what prize-winning essay?

A. "The Farmyard."

Q. What Pennsylvania city was home to such newspapers as the *Log Cabin Rifle, Plough Boy, Magician,* and *Yeoman* during the 1830s and 1840s?

A. Harrisburg.

Q. Rita Mae Brown wrote what book that partly took place in York County?

A. *Rubyfruit Jungle.*

Q. What Lumberville-born painter in 1864 was made a Knight of the Order of the Rose by Emperor Don Pedro II of Brazil?

A. Martin Johnson Head.

Q. In 1929, what writer born in Bethlehem in 1898 received the Pulitzer Prize for poetry for his book *John Brown's Body*?

A. Stephen Vincent Benét.

Q. Who organized the Philadelphia Orchestra in 1900?

A. Fritz Scheel.

Q. German-born and Philadelphia-schooled painter Emanuel G. Leutze used what river as a model for his work *Washington Crossing the Delaware*?

A. Rhine River, Germany.

Q. What Harrisburg organization, originally founded as a cooking club, changed its direction in 1882 to promote community musical awareness?

A. The Wednesday Club.

Q. What Bucks County carpenter painted the folk art masterpiece *Manchester Valley*?

A. Joseph Pickett.

Q. Novelist Mary Roberts Rinehart published her autobiography under what title?

A. *My Story.*

Q. What recipient of the 1938 Nobel Prize for literature lived with her children on a farm in Bucks County for a number of years?

A. Pearl S. Buck.

Q. In 1962 Springdale-born writer Rachel Carson published what eye-opening blockbuster on dangers to the environment?

A. *Silent Spring.*

Q. In 1865 what Philadelphia periodical was the largest labor journal in America?

A. *Fincher's Trade Review.*

Q. What Allegheny-born writer produced such works as *The Making of Americans, Tender Button,* and *The Autobiography of Alice B. Toklas*?

A. Gertrude Stein.

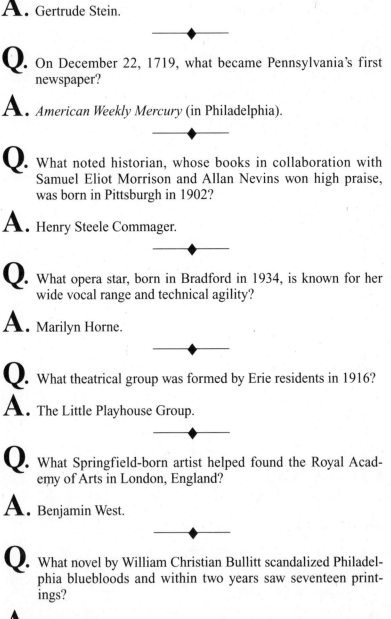

Q. On December 22, 1719, what became Pennsylvania's first newspaper?

A. *American Weekly Mercury* (in Philadelphia).

Q. What noted historian, whose books in collaboration with Samuel Eliot Morrison and Allan Nevins won high praise, was born in Pittsburgh in 1902?

A. Henry Steele Commager.

Q. What opera star, born in Bradford in 1934, is known for her wide vocal range and technical agility?

A. Marilyn Horne.

Q. What theatrical group was formed by Erie residents in 1916?

A. The Little Playhouse Group.

Q. What Springfield-born artist helped found the Royal Academy of Arts in London, England?

A. Benjamin West.

Q. What novel by William Christian Bullitt scandalized Philadelphia bluebloods and within two years saw seventeen printings?

A. *It's Not Done.*

Q. Philadelphian Anthony Faas patented what musical instrument in 1854?

A. The accordion.

◆

Q. What 1,224-page historical novel, written in 1933 by Pittsburgh-born writer Hervey Allen, was translated into eighteen foreign languages?

A. *Anthony Adverse.*

◆

Q. In 1930 what McKeesport writer not only won a Pulitzer Prize for drama for *Coroner's Inquest* but also an O'Henry award?

A. Marc Connelly.

◆

Q. What early American portrait painter was born at Downingtown in 1776?

A. Jacob Eichholtz.

◆

Q. What novel by Charles Brockden Brown gave a firsthand description of the Philadelphia yellow fever epidemic of 1793?

A. *Arthur Mervyn.*

◆

Q. What Pittsburgh-born actress appeared in such Broadway plays as *Major Barbara, Rhinoceros,* and *The Diary of Anne Frank?*

A. Anne Jackson.

◆

Q. What was Pennsylvania-born writer Louisa May Alcott's first book?

A. *Flower Fables* (1854).

Q. Agnes Sligh Turnbull, who was born in the community of New Alexandria, is best known for what 1947 novel?

A. *The Bishop's Mantle.*

Q. What nineteenth-century, Edgeworth-born composer penned such works as "The Rosary," "Narcissus," and "A Day in Venice"?

A. Ethelbert Nevin.

Q. Beginning publication in Philadelphia in January 1775, what was the first evening newspaper in Pennsylvania?

A. *Pennsylvania Evening Post.*

Q. What Philadelphia-born composer/conductor wrote such songs as "Heart to Heart," "Sugartown Road," and "Once upon a Moon"?

A. Elliot Lawrence.

Q. What principal dancer for the American Ballet Theatre, who contributed to the renaissance of ballet in the United States, was born in Bethlehem in 1952?

A. Gelsey Kirkland.

Q. What $2.1 million playhouse was constructed in Pittsburgh in 1903?

A. The Nixon Theater.

Q. What was Bayard Taylor's first poem, which appeared in the *Saturday Evening Post* in 1839?

A. "Soliloquy of a Young Poet."

Q. What is the English translation of Bethlehem's first newspaper, *Die Bien,* published in German in 1847?

A. "The Bee."

Q. For what Philadelphia magazine did Edgar Allan Poe work as an editor for three years?

A. *Graham's Magazine.*

Q. What satirical ballad by Philadelphia lawyer Francis Hopkinson so outraged the British that redcoat soldiers set fire to his home?

A. "The Battle of the Kegs."

Q. At the beginning of the nineteenth century, proponents of Jeffersonian democracy founded what publication in Pittsburgh?

A. *Tree of Knowledge.*

Q. Reading's first newspaper in 1789 was a German publication of what title?

A. *Zeitung.*

Q. Who in 1926 founded the Workers' Theater Alliance in Philadelphia?

A. Alfred Sobel.

Q. Born in Johnstown in 1881, what Pennsylvania composer is best known for "At Dawning" and "The Land of Sky-blue Water"?

A. Charles Wakefield Cadman.

Q. What nineteenth-century Pennsylvania newspaper headed by Sarah C. F. Hallowell was staffed entirely by women?

A. *New Century.*

Q. What author of romantic novels (many illustrated by Charles Dana Gibson) and the best-known reporter and war correspondent of his generation was born in Philadelphia in 1864?

A. Richard Harding Davis.

Q. Kyle Crichton, who was born in Peale, wrote articles for the *Daily Worker* and the *New Masses* using what pen name?

A. Robert Forsythe.

Q. What was the lengthy name of Philadelphia's second newspaper, which made its debut on December 24, 1728?

A. *Universal Instructor in All the Sciences and Pennsylvania Gazette.*

Q. What pop artist and multimedia innovator, known for his avant-garde film *L'Etoile de Mer,* was born in Philadelphia in 1890?

A. Man Ray.

Q. The Moravians at Bethlehem formed what organization in 1744 to cultivate secular and church music?

A. Collegium Musicum.

Q. What Philadelphia-born poet, children's author, and fiction writer won the 1973 Pulitzer Prize for poetry for *Up Country*?

A. Maxine Kumin.

SPORTS & LEISURE

Q. In 1935 what Pennsylvania university team met Tulane in the first Sugar Bowl?

A. Glenn "Pop" Warner's Temple University Owls.

Q. What name is given to the popular Italian bowling game played in South Philly?

A. Bocce.

Q. Pittsburgh Pirates Paul and Lloyd Waner were known by what nicknames?

A. Big Poison and Little Poison.

Q. In 1980 what sports museum was moved from Los Angeles, California, to York, Pennsylvania?

A. Weightlifters Hall of Fame.

Q. The Philadelphia Flyers defeated what team in the 1974–75 Stanley Cup finals?

A. Boston Sabres.

Q. What Philadelphia native started his career as a third baseman, then spent fourteen years as a star pitcher in the big leagues?

A. Bucky Walters.

Q. In 1930 what internationally famous golfer captured the U.S. Amateur title at the Merion Cricket Club in Ardmore?

A. Bobby Jones.

Q. Punxsutawney is nationally known for celebrating what event?

A. Groundhog Day, February 2.

Q. What major league shortstop for seventeen seasons died in Philadelphia on September 12, 1993, at age sixty-six?

A. Granville Hamner.

Q. By scoring forty-six points, what Penn State basketball player went into the record books at the all-time leader in a single game?

A. Gene Harris (against Holy Cross, 1962).

Q. What Egypt native pitched twenty years in the major leagues?

A. Curt Simmons.

Q. York is the home of what factory manufacturing the only motorcycle still made in the United States?

A. Harley-Davidson.

Q. What professional arena football team organized in Pittsburgh?

A. Pittsburgh Gladiators.

───────◆───────

Q. What Pittsburgh pitcher led the 1979 world champion Pirates with only fourteen victories?

A. John Candelaria.

───────◆───────

Q. What boxer, famed for his 1941 heavyweight title bout against Joe Louis, died in Pittsburgh on May 19, 1993, at age seventy-five?

A. Billy Conn.

───────◆───────

Q. Famed quarterback Johnny Unitas joined what professional football team in 1955, only to be released before the season opener?

A. Pittsburgh Steelers.

───────◆───────

Q. The Meadows in Washington County is a facility for what type of horse racing?

A. Harness racing.

───────◆───────

Q. What Philadelphia Phillies moundsman delivered the last pitch to Babe Ruth in his big-league career?

A. Jim Bivin.

───────◆───────

Q. Between 1946 and 1962 what professional basketball team made Philadelphia its home?

A. Philadelphia Warriors.

Q. Who became the first Pittsburgh Steeler to rush for one thousand yards in one season?

A. John Henry Johnson.

Q. What are the colors of Temple University?

A. Cherry and white.

Q. Philadelphia native Wilt Chamberlain set an NBA single game scoring record in Hershey Park Arena on March 2, 1962, recording how many points?

A. One hundred.

Q. What sports author, columnist, and TV commentator died in Pittsburgh on February 2, 1990, at age forty-seven?

A. Pete Axthelm.

Q. Winning 147 games and losing 73 in seventeen years, who was named the first formal basketball coach at Penn State?

A. Burke M. "Dutch" Hermann.

Q. What famous NFL quarterback was born in Youngwood?

A. George Blanda.

Q. The terrain of Somerset County provides what four ski areas?

A. Seven Springs, Hidden Valley, Kings Mountain, and Laurel Mountain.

Q. What Wyncote-born power hitter holds the major league record for career strikeouts?

A. Reggie Jackson (2,597).

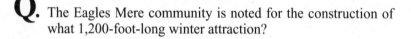

Q. Singer Kate Smith referred to what Philadelphia team as "my boys"?

A. The Flyers.

Q. The Eagles Mere community is noted for the construction of what 1,200-foot-long winter attraction?

A. The Lake Avenue toboggan slide.

Q. In 1987 what two Pittsburgh Steelers were inducted into the Pro Football Hall of Fame?

A. Joe Greene and John Henry Johnson.

Q. What Temple University basketball player was the state's leading scorer as a senior at Morrisville High School?

A. Mike Vreeswyk.

Q. The Associated Press designated what Latrobe native Athlete of the Decade in 1970?

A. Arnold Palmer.

Q. New Castle-born Harvey Harmon was once the president of what famous sports organization?

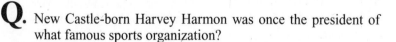

A. The Pro Football Hall of Fame.

Q. In what year did the Penn State Nittany Lions first become national football champions?

A. 1982.

Q. In 1962 what player was the number one draft pick of the Philadelphia Warriors?

A. Wayne Hightower of Kansas.

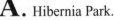

Q. Where was the first American Legion Junior World Series held?

A. Squa Centennial Stadium, Philadelphia (1926).

Q. What Pennsylvania-born player spent twenty-two years with the St. Louis Cardinals, winning the National League batting championship seven times?

A. Stan Musial.

Q. The Old Fiddlers' Picnic is hosted by what Chester County park on the second Saturday in August?

A. Hibernia Park.

Q. What small, light racing boat, either one-man or crew, is a familiar sight skimming over the Schuylkill River?

A. A scull.

Q. Who became the first Phillies player ever to attain double figures in doubles, triples, homers, and stolen bases his first four years in the big leagues?

A. Juan Samuel.

Q. What Factoryville-born major league pitcher was victorious over twelve opponents simultaneously in chess matches at the Pittsburgh Athletic Club?

A. Christy Mathewson.

Q. Potter County annually sponsors what difficult long distance run in June?

A. God's Country Marathon.

Q. What National Football League team folded due to the Great Depression, only to be reactivated in 1933 as the Philadelphia Eagles?

A. The Frankford Yellow Jackets.

Q. Near Trexlertown, what is one of only about a dozen active bicycle tracks in the country?

A. Lehigh County Velodrome.

Q. What great rebounder for the University of Pittsburgh continued an athletic career as defensive lineman for the Cleveland Browns?

A. Sam Clancy.

Q. What 1993 baseball Hall of Famer excelled at Cheltenham High School in track, football, and baseball?

A. Reggie Jackson.

Q. What Philadelphia 76er is a cousin to the former NBA player Jeff Judkins?

A. Danny Vranes.

Q. Olympic and National AAU Weightlifting Champion and Mr. Universe were titles won by what York resident?

A. Bill March.

Q. What Philadelphia 76er was known by the nickname "Mad Dog"?

A. Fred Carter.

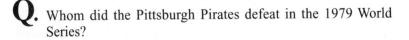

Q. Whom did the Pittsburgh Pirates defeat in the 1979 World Series?

A. Baltimore Orioles.

Q. What is the name of the youth hockey organization sponsored by the Philadelphia Flyers?

A. Hockey Central.

Q. What University of Pittsburgh basketball player led the NCAA in rebounding for the 1986–87 season?

A. Jerome Lane.

Q. The Phillies met the Boston Red Sox at what site in the 1915 World Series?

A. Baker Bowl (Philadelphia).

Q. What Penn State quarterback finished second to Billy Cannon of Louisiana State in balloting for the 1959 Heisman Trophy?

A. Rich Lucas.

Q. What founder of Little League baseball died in Williamsport on June 4, 1922, at age eighty-two?

A. Carl Stotz.

Q. Who was the only member of the 1986 season Philadelphia Eagle offensive line to start all sixteen games?

A. Ron Baker.

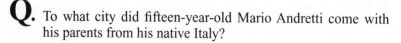

Q. To what city did fifteen-year-old Mario Andretti come with his parents from his native Italy?

A. Nazareth.

Q. The Comeback Player of the Year Award was presented to what Pittsburgh Pirate in 1985?

A. Rick Reuschel.

Q. With 714 points, who was the scoring leader for Temple University ending the 1986–87 basketball season?

A. Nate Blackwell.

Q. What is the seating capacity of Penn State's Beaver Stadium?

A. 93,967.

Q. Glen Mills is noted for having the first manufacturing plant for what item?

A. Roller skates.

Q. Former President Eisenhower named what Marcus Hook native his favorite baseball player?

A. Mickey Vernon.

◆

Q. The streetlights in "Chocolate Town, U.S.A" are designed in the shape of what confectionary delight?

A. Hershey's Kisses.

◆

Q. In 1939 the Pittsburgh Steelers signed what Colorado All-American, later U.S. Supreme Court justice?

A. Byron "Whizzer" White.

◆

Q. What Pennsylvania college was the smallest school ever to be invited to the Rose Bowl?

A. Washington and Jefferson College (1922).

◆

Q. In what year did Mike Schmidt win the World Series Most Valuable Player award?

A. 1980.

◆

Q. What Pittsburgh-born NFL quarterback led the Baltimore Colts to three world championships?

A. Johnny Unitas.

◆

Q. What Pittsburgh Pirate led the National League in home runs for the seven seasons he played for the team (1946–52)?

A. Ralph Kiner.

Q. How many water related rides are in Hershey Park?

A. Five.

◆

Q. During the 1987 season, what Philadelphia Philly tied a National League record collecting the winning RBI in four consecutive games?

A. Milt Thompson.

◆

Q. As of 1994, what is the ratio of World Series wins between Philadelphia and Pittsburgh?

A. 5:5.

◆

Q. Lawrence County basketball great Charles "Horse" Gillium of the late 1920s was one of a few ballplayers who could perform what trick?

A. Palming two basketballs simultaneously with arms outstretched.

◆

Q. University of Pittsburgh football player Bill Fralic attained All-Pro status while playing for what team?

A. Atlanta Falcons.

◆

Q. On May 22, 1952, what Phillies pitcher hit an inside-the-park home run?

A. Curt Simmons.

◆

Q. The nation's largest indoor tennis tournament is held annually at what Pennsylvania sports facility?

A. The Spectrum in Philadelphia.

Q. On November 25, 1975, Liberty Bell Park in Philadelphia introduced what sports "first" in the nation?

A. Harness racing measured in metric distances.

Q. What Pennsylvania team lost the Little League World Series in 1947 but won it in 1948?

A. Lock Haven.

Q. Penn State All-American Glenn Ressler became an All-Pro guard for what professional team?

A. Baltimore Colts.

Q. What Philadelphia Phillies shortstop was selected to play in five All-Star games between 1974 and 1979?

A. Larry Bowa.

Q. How many consecutive times did Wilt Chamberlain have a 2,000-or-more point season?

A. Seven.

Q. Philadelphia socialite Anthony J. Drexel Biddle Sr., an author and amateur boxer, founded what organization in which boxing and Bible classes were combined?

A. Athletic Christianity.

Q. What top-ranking NASCAR facility is located at Long Pond?

A. Pocono International Raceway.

Q. What Pennsylvania team is considered to have been the greatest black baseball team ever assembled?

A. The Pittsburgh Crawfords.

Q. The Cy Young Award for 1990 went to what National League player?

A. Doug Drabek, Pittsburgh Pirates.

Q. In what year did the Army-Navy football classic first take place in Philadelphia?

A. 1899.

Q. What sport played in the cities of Pennsylvania is a cross between rugby and soccer?

A. Gaelic football.

Q. In the spring of 1963 what professional basketball team was brought to Philadelphia to be renamed the 76ers?

A. Syracuse Nats.

———◆———

Q. In what sport was James Hazen of Lawrence County a world class participant?

A. Gymnastics.

———◆———

Q. In 1982 the University of Pittsburgh's basketball program announced it would become the ninth member of what conference?

A. Big East Conference.

Q. In 1987 what Villanova basketball player became the first athlete in the school's history to be named to the Kodak All-American team?

A. Shelly Pennefather.

———◆———

Q. In what city was the first National League game ever played?

A. Philadelphia.

———◆———

Q. On May 25, 1935, what Pittsburgh pitcher gave up the two final home runs of Babe Ruth's major league career?

A. Guy Bush.

———◆———

Q. In 1884 Philadelphian LeMarcus Thompson created what amusement ride for thrill seekers?

A. The roller-coaster.

———◆———

Q. In 1994, what former Philadelphia Phillies lefthander was chosen for the Baseball Hall of Fame his first year of eligibility?

A. Steve Carlton.

———◆———

Q. "Buzz" Guy, who played for the NFL's Giants, Cowboys, and Broncos, began his football career at what Lawrence County high school?

A. Ellwood City.

———◆———

Q. What Pittsburgh Pirate was the only rookie pitcher to win three games in a World Series?

A. Babe Adams (1909).

Q. In the 1951 heavyweight championship of the world, Jersey Joe Walcott upset what opponent in Pittsburgh?

A. Ezzard Charles.

Q. What NFL team was first to receive the Vince Lombardi trophy three times?

A. Pittsburgh Steelers.

Q. The Villanova Wildcats won the NCAA basketball national championship in what year?

A. 1985.

Q. On October 13, 1971, what Pittsburgh Pirates pitcher threw the first pitch in a World Series night game?

A. Luke Walker.

Q. What two consecutive seasons did the Pittsburgh Penguins win the Stanley Cup?

A. 1990–91 and 1991–92.

Q. What team did Penn State beat, 42–17, in the 1992 Fiesta Bowl?

A. Tennessee.

Q. Inaugurated on June 30, 1909, what Pennsylvania sports facility was the first steel-structured stadium to be built?

A. Forbes Field, Pittsburgh.

Q. On May 26, 1959, what Pittsburgh pitcher hurled twelve perfect innings only to lose to the Braves in the thirteenth, 1–0?

A. Harvey Haddix.

Q. In a career of twenty-three years, Steelers coach Chuck Noll won how many games?

A. 209.

Q. In 1987 what Pittsburgh Pirate received the National League's Gold Glove Award?

A. Mike LaValliere.

Q. What former Olympic medal winner closed his fourteen-year NFL career as a running back with the Eagles, 1964–66?

A. Ollie Matson.

Q. Stan Musial set a major league record by hitting how many home runs in a doubleheader?

A. Five.

Q. Phillie Lenny Dykstra tied in 1990 for the National League's leader in hits, with 192, but won the honor alone in 1993 with how many hits?

A. 194.

Q. The Pittsburgh Pirates played their first National League game in what year?

A. 1887.

Q. Johnny Unitas set a record for throwing touchdown passes in how many consecutive games?

A. Forty-seven.

Q. Bucknell University in Lewisburg plays in what NCAA basketball conference?

A. Patriot.

Q. What college fielded the spring 1994 men's volleyball championship team?

A. Penn State.

Q. At one time Pittsburgh was home for what ABA basketball league franchise?

A. Pittsburgh Condors.

Q. In 1993, what shortstop won the National Leagues Gold Glove Award, supplanting Cardinal Ozzie Smith, who had won it every year since 1979?

A. Pittsburgh Pirate Jay Bell.

Q. What one-time Philadelphia Phillies player (1921) became head coach of the Philadelphia Eagles, 1941–50?

A. Greasy Neale.

Q. With 5,611 hits, what brother duo had more hits than any other brother combination in baseball history?

A. Lloyd and Paul Waner.

Q. What left-handed pitcher born in Kennett Square won 240 games and participated in five World Series?

A. Herb Pennock.

◆

Q. The Philadelphia Eagles retired jersey number 15 belonging to what outstanding running back?

A. Steve Van Buren.

◆

Q. What Carlisle Indians teammate was called by Coach Glenn "Pop" Warner "the greatest football player of all time"?

A. Jim Thorpe.

◆

Q. How many times did Pittsburgh Pirate Honus Wagner win the National League batting championship?

A. Eight.

◆

Q. What Philadelphia Flyer was the only National Hockey League rookie selected to the All-Star team for the Rendez-Vous '87 series?

A. Ron Hextall.

◆

Q. In what Delaware County house museum is displayed a jar of sawdust from Billy Sunday's "sawdust trail" and sand from the digging of the Panama Canal?

A. The Christian C. Sanderson Museum.

◆

Q. In 1836 what Pennsylvania school witnessed the first cricket game played by a college team?

A. Haverford College.

Q. In 1978 the Pittsburgh Steelers defeated what club, 35–31, in Super Bowl XIII?

A. Dallas Cowboys.

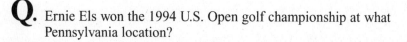

Q. Ernie Els won the 1994 U.S. Open golf championship at what Pennsylvania location?

A. Oakmont Country Club.

Q. What was the first indoor sport played at Penn State?

A. Basketball (1897).

Q. Penn State defeated what team, 27–23, in the 1982 Sugar Bowl?

A. Georgia.

Q. What baseball club has the oldest team name in the National League?

A. The Phillies (1883).

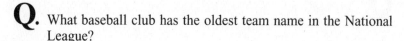

Q. What Penn State fencer was the collegiate individual fencing champion for two consecutive years?

A. Olga Kalinovskaya, 1993 and 1994.

Q. *ABC's Wide World of Sports* presented what Philadelphia event on its premiere telecast?

A. The Penn Relays.

Q. In consecutive years what two Pittsburgh Pirates were chosen the National League's Most Valuable Player but were not selected to play in the All-Star game?

A. Dave Parker (1978) and Willie Stargell (1979).

◆

Q. Penn, Princeton, and Columbia Universities compete for what trophy every third year on the Schuylkill River?

A. The Child Cup.

◆

Q. What Pittsburgh Penguin player was the first to score four goals in a single game?

A. Paul Gardner.

◆

Q. What September festivity at the Mount Hope estate near Marietta features jousting and Elizabethan delicacies?

A. Pennsylvania Renaissance Faire.

◆

Q. In 1945 what Philadelphian won the pro doubles championship with Vincent Richards at age fifty-two?

A. William T. Tilden Jr.

◆

Q. The Municipal Stadium (now J.F.K. Stadium) in South Philadelphia was the site of what renowned heavyweight boxing match?

A. The Dempsy-Tunney fight.

◆

Q. What Pittsburgh Pirate holds the distinction of being the only major league ball player to end a World Series with a home run?

A. Bill Mazeroski (Game 7, 1960 World Series).

Q. For two consecutive years what Pittsburgh Penguin won the Art Ross Trophy for leading the NHL in scoring points during the regular season?

A. Mario Lemieux (1992, 1993).

Q. The Pennsylvania high school golf championships of 1946 and 1947 were won by what now-famous pro golfer?

A. Arnold Palmer.

Q. What former University of Pittsburgh football player became an All-Pro guard with the Washington Redskins?

A. Russ Grimm.

Q. Who ranks as the 76ers' top career leader in turnovers?

A. Julius Erving.

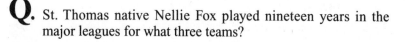

Q. St. Thomas native Nellie Fox played nineteen years in the major leagues for what three teams?

A. Philadelphia A's, Chicago White Sox, and Houston Astros.

Q. York native Linda Ann Myers was at one time world champion of what sport?

A. Archery.

Q. What Pittsburgh manager led the Pirates to four eastern division crowns and two World Series championships (1960 and 1971)?

A. Danny Murtaugh.

Q. On April 18, 1987, Mike Schmidt hit his five-hundredth home run off what pitcher?

A. Don Robinson (Pittsburgh).

———◆———

Q. After Pittsburgh Pirates outfield Barry Bonds was named the National League's Most Valuable Player for 1990, he received the same honor in 1992 and 1993 as a player for what team?

A. San Francisco Giants.

———◆———

Q. Who is known as the father of the Pittsburgh Steelers?

A. Arthur Joseph Rooney.

———◆———

Q. The Davey O'Brien award, presented to the nation's number one quarterback, was given to what Penn State player in 1982?

A. Todd Blackledge.

———◆———

Q. Little League baseball was started in what Pennsylvania community?

A. Williamsport.

———◆———

Q. Specialty shops, ethnic foods, and entertainment facilities are all part of what downtown Harrisburg complex?

A. Strawberry Square.

———◆———

Q. The Pittsburgh Steelers and the Philadelphia Eagles merged in 1943 playing under what name?

A. Steagles.

Q. Having originated in Philadelphia, what is the oldest nickname used by any major league ball club?

A. Athletics or A's.

———◆———

Q. Foxburg in northwest Pennsylvania is home for what sports museum?

A. The American Golf Hall of Fame.

———◆———

Q. What nickname was given to Reggie Jackson due to his performances in World Series contests?

A. "Mr. October."

———◆———

Q. In the 1993–94 season, what basketball player was the individual scoring leader of the NCAA women's division II?

A. Tammy Greene, Philadelphia College of Textiles and Science, with 782 points.

———◆———

Q. How many Pittsburgh Pirates runners were left on base—one shy of the National League record for a nine-inning game—when they lost, 6–4, to the Philadelphia Phillies on May 12, 1994?

A. Seventeen.

———◆———

Q. What two-time All-American University of Pittsburgh basketball player set a school record by scoring forty-five points against Duke in 1958?

A. Don Hennon.

———◆———

Q. Although it maintained the "Phillies" title, what nickname was given the Philadelphia ball club during 1944 and 1945?

A. The Blue Jays.

Q. What famous major league shortstop operated a sporting goods store in Pittsburgh following his playing days?

A. Honus Wagner.

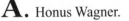

Q. On July 1, 1994, who were the first brothers in major league history to get saves on the same night?

A. Josias Manzanillos of the New York Mets and Ravelo Manzanillos of the Pittsburgh Pirates.

Q. What left-handed pitcher, born in Bradford, won 191 games in thirteen years in the majors?

A. Rube Waddell.

Q. Winning 126 consecutive sculling races during 1919–20, what Philadelphian was named America's All-Time Sculling Champ?

A. John B. Kelly (father of actress Grace Kelly).

Q. What award is given annually to the outstanding player of the Penn State-Pittsburgh football game?

A. James Coogan Award.

Q. What famous 1980s car was built by New Castle native Chuck Lombardo?

A. ZZ Top Coupe.

Q. Who served as the Pittsburgh Penguins team captain during the 1986–87 season?

A. Terry Ruskowski.

Q. The Phillies baseball club won the World Series in what year?

A. 1980.

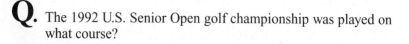

Q. The 1992 U.S. Senior Open golf championship was played on what course?

A. Saucon Valley Country Club (Bethlehem).

Q. What Pittsburgh Pirate is the only man to have hit a ball out of Dodger Stadium?

A. Willie Stargell (on two occasions).

Q. On August 5, 1921, what Pennsylvania radio station was the first ever to broadcast a baseball game?

A. KDKA, Pittsburgh (Pirates vs. Phillies).

Q. Who was chosen by Philadelphia fans in 1983 as the greatest Phillies player ever?

A. Mike Schmidt.

Q. After scoring two goals in the 1975 NHL All-Star game in Montreal, what Pittsburgh Penguin was named Most Valuable Player?

A. Syl Apps.

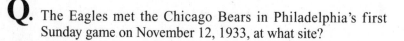

Q. The Eagles met the Chicago Bears in Philadelphia's first Sunday game on November 12, 1933, at what site?

A. Baker Bowl, Philadelphia.

Q. Penn State lost, 60–58, to what team in the 1965 NCAA basketball tournament?

A. Princeton.

Q. What Philadelphia Philly is the brother of a running back for the New England Patriots?

A. Chris James (brother of Craig).

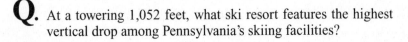

Q. At a towering 1,052 feet, what ski resort features the highest vertical drop among Pennsylvania's skiing facilities?

A. Blue Knob.

Q. What well-known Pittsburgh third baseman was elected to the Hall of Fame in 1948?

A. Harold "Pie" Traynor.

Q. What was Jim Thorpe's full name?

A. James Francis Thorpe.

Q. Thoroughbred racing takes place at what popular Erie facility?

A. Commodore Downs.

Q. In what year did Honus Wagner become the first Pittsburgh Pirate named to the Hall of Fame?

A. 1936.

Q. Blair Thomas ran for how many yards against Syracuse in 1986, setting a Penn State record?

A. Ninety-two.

Q. What fourteen-year major league pitcher born in Plains was elected to the Baseball Hall of Fame in 1946?

A. "Big Ed" Walsh.

Q. What American Hockey League franchise operates out of the greater Harrisburg area?

A. Hershey Bears.

Q. On April 11, 1970, what Pittsburgh Penguin recorded the only playoff hat trick in the club's history?

A. Ken Schinkel.

Q. What Pittsburgh Steeler became the first strong safety in the history of the NFL to intercept fifty passes?

A. Donnie Shell.

Q. Three Rivers Stadium is located in what city?

A. Pittsburgh.

Q. What Philadelphia Eagle running back was the second leading rusher in Ohio State history behind Archie Griffin?

A. Keith Byars.

Q. What Pittsburgh-born shortstop commanded baseball's highest salary in 1906 at $6,500?

A. Bobby Wallace.

Q. Upon completion of his collegiate career in 1975, what Temple University left-footed placekicker had established five NCAA all-time records?

A. Don Bitterlich.

Q. What two Pennsylvania town teams faced each other in the first professional football game on September 3, 1895?

A. Latrobe vs. Jeannette.

Q. The Pittsburgh Steelers made their first postseason appearances in what year?

A. 1947.

Q. What Ellwood City-born outfielder holds the major league record for RBI's at 190?

A. Hack Wilson, 1930.

Q. What Penn State basketball player made All-American in 1955?

A. Jesse Arnelle.

Q. What University of Pennsylvania football player scored three touchdowns against Navy in the October 18, 1986, game?

A. Brent Novoselsky.

Q. What Waynesboro native played second base on Connie Mack's Philadelphia Athletics in the 1929–31 World Series?

A. Max Bishop.

Q. Penn State produced what Heisman Trophy winner in 1973?

A. John Cappelletti.

Q. What National League baseball club participated in the first World Series in 1903?

A. Pittsburgh Pirates.

Q. In 1986 and 1987 what Villanova basketball player was named to first team Academic All-American honors?

A. Harold Jensen.

Q. Where was the former professional football star Joe Namath born?

A. Beaver Falls.

---◆---

Q. What sport facility in Pennsylvania was the site of the first ever football telecast?

A. Franklin Field, Philadelphia (Philco, October 5, 1939).

---◆---

Q. What 76er won his first NBA rebounding title during the 1986–87 campaign with a 14.6 average?

A. Charles Barkley.

Q. What Shamokin-born pitcher made the Baseball Hall of Fame in 1969?

A. Stan Coveleski.

———◆———

Q. In 1948 the Philadelphia Eagles won their first NFL championship defeating what team in a blinding snowstorm at Shibe Park?

A. Chicago Cardinals (7–0).

———◆———

Q. Where is the oldest golf course in continuous use in the United States?

A. Foxburg.

———◆———

Q. What Pittsburgh Penguin recorded the club's first shutout on November 4, 1967?

A. Les Binkley.

———◆———

Q. At what Westmoreland County museum will one find a large selection of firearms dating back to 1450?

A. Forbes Road Gun Museum.

———◆———

Q. Eight baseball teams formed what major league at Philadelphia in 1900?

A. The American League.

———◆———

Q. What city hosts the annual AAABA Baseball Tournament, known to many as the best amateur baseball contest in the world?

A. Johnstown (Point Stadium).

Q. The 1986 Asa S. Bushnell Cup, given to the Ivy League's top football player, was awarded to what University of Pennsylvania athlete?

A. Rich Comizio.

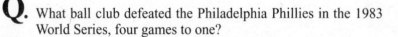

Q. How many years did Wilkinsburg native Bill McKechnie manage in the major leagues?

A. Twenty-five.

Q. What type of sporting event was broadcast for the first time on radio on August 4, 1921, from Sewickley?

A. A tennis match.

Q. In what Pennsylvania community was the legendary shortstop Honus Wagner born?

A. Carnegie.

Q. What ball club defeated the Philadelphia Phillies in the 1983 World Series, four games to one?

A. Baltimore Orioles.

Q. Who was the first player in the history of the Pittsburgh Penguins to record two consecutive one hundred-point seasons?

A. Mario Lemieux.

Q. What famous Pittsburgh Pirate shortstop won the batting championship in 1935 with a .385 average?

A. Joseph "Arky" Vaughn.

Q. Boston faced what Pennsylvania team in the first National League game on April 22, 1876?

A. Philadelphia Athletics.

———◆———

Q. What individual was selected Sportsman of the Year by *Sports Illustrated* magazine in 1986?

A. Penn State head football coach Joe Paterno.

———◆———

Q. How many times was Phillies pitcher Steve Carlton presented the National League's Cy Young Award?

A. Four: 1972, 1977, 1980, and 1982.

———◆———

Q. During the 1951–53 campaigns, what Penn Quaker led the basketball team in career points scored?

A. Ernest Beck (1,827).

———◆———

Q. What Brookville-born pitcher played in five World Series and later coached baseball at Dartmouth College?

A. Bob Shawkey.

———◆———

Q. In 1983 fans selected what three outfielders to be named to the all-time greatest Philadelphia Phillies team?

A. Richie Ashburn, Garry Maddox, and Del Ennis.

———◆———

Q. Philadelphia-born Jimmy Wilson spent eighteen years in the big leagues at what position?

A. Catcher.

Q. On June 27, 1930, just eight days short of his forty-sixth birthday, what Philadelphia Athletics pitcher became the oldest player in the history of the big leagues to hit a home run?

A. Jack Quinn.

Q. What Penn State linebacker retired in 1984 after an All-Pro career with the Pittsburgh Steelers?

A. Jack Ham.

Q. In 1981 what University of Pittsburgh quarterback was selected first team All-America?

A. Dan Marino.

Q. On July 6, 1980, Pittsburgh defeated Chicago, 5–4, in the longest game played at Three Rivers Stadium, totaling how many innings?

A. Twenty.

Q. Who captained the University of Pennsylvania's 1898 football team?

A. John Outland (for whom the Outland Trophy is named).

Q. What Philadelphia Philly ended the 1987 season leading the team in pinch hits for the seventh time?

A. Greg Gross.

Q. In 1962 what three Pittsburgh Pirates were named to the National League All-Star squad as starters?

A. Roberto Clemente, Dick Groat, and Bill Mazeroski.

Q. United Press International named what Penn State linebacker to the 1986 first team All-America?

A. Shane Conlan.

Q. What was the original name of baseball great Connie Mack?

A. Cornelius McGillicuddy.

Q. While a resident of Mount Airy, Pennsylvania, Charles Darrow invented what famous board game?

A. Monopoly.

Q. Ed Pinckney of Villanova moved to what NBA team following his 1985–87 career with Phoenix?

A. Sacramento.

Q. What Phillies player set the club's rookie record in 1982 by stealing forty-two bases?

A. Bob Dernier.

Q. Who became the first Pittsburgh Penguin to score fifty goals in one season?

A. Jean Pronovost.

Q. During what years did the legendary John W. Heisman coach at the University of Pennsylvania?

A. 1920–22.

SCIENCE & NATURE

C H A P T E R S I X

Q. Who drilled Pennsylvania's first oil well near Titusville in 1859?

A. Col. Edwin L. Drake.

◆

Q. At the 1876 World's Fair, a Philadelphia pharmacist concocted and sold packages of herbs, bark, and roots to be brewed into what new soft drink?

A. Hires root beer.

◆

Q. What tasty fruit and dairy product was first produced at Troy in 1808?

A. Pineapple cheese.

◆

Q. A grave-robbing episode by a local doctor at Brookville in 1857 eventually resulted in the passage of what type of legislation in Pennsylvania?

A. The legalization of dissecting human cadavers.

◆

Q. In 1889 Middletown was the site of what Joshua Pusey invention?

A. Book matches.

Q. In 1763 what Lancaster resident built the first steamboat in America, only to see it fail when tested?

A. William Henry.

Q. Geologically, what area in Pennsylvania is considered to be the oldest?

A. The Piedmont Plateau.

Q. Around 1850 what disease contracted from dogs virtually exterminated all the wolves in Pennsylvania?

A. Hydrophobia.

Q. What is the official Pennsylvania state animal?

A. Whitetail deer.

Q. In 1898 Pennsylvania first purchased land for the conservation and reclamation of what natural resource?

A. Forests.

Q. The first medical school in the country opened in 1765 in what educational institution?

A. The College and Academy of Philadelphia, now the University of Pennsylvania.

Q. Where is the Bark Peelers' Convention held each July?

A. Pennsylvania Lumber Museum, Coudersport.

Q. What University of Pennsylvania researcher developed the much-publicized Retin-A for acne treatment and sun-damaged skin restoration?

A. Dr. Albert Klingman.

———◆———

Q. What sanctuary for birds of prey was established at Eckville in 1934?

A. Hawk Mountain Bird Sanctuary.

———◆———

Q. Where was Pennsylvania's first state park created in 1893?

A. Valley Forge.

———◆———

Q. What anthropologist, who served in 1975 as president of the American Association for the Advancement of Science, was born in Philadelphia in 1901?

A. Margaret Mead.

———◆———

Q. What is the only species of bear found in the Commonwealth?

A. Black bear.

———◆———

Q. The polio vaccine was discovered by Dr. Jonas Salk while he was teaching at what Pennsylvania institution of higher learning?

A. University of Pittsburgh.

———◆———

Q. What record low temperature was recorded in Smethport (McKean County) on January 5, 1904?

A. $-42°$ F.

Q. What organization was formed by Caroline Earle White at Philadelphia in 1883 to bring attention to the poor treatment of research animals?

A. The American Anti-Vivisection Society.

Q. The 1901 General Artificial Silk Company in Lansdowne invented what synthetic fiber?

A. Rayon.

Q. Where can one see the tumor removed from President Grover Cleveland's jaw in 1893?

A. The Mutter Museum of the College of Physicians of Philadelphia.

Q. What is the official state bird?

A. Ruffled grouse.

Q. What state mental health agency was established in 1883?

A. The Committee on Lunacy.

Q. What unique natural phenomenon was discovered in 1894 near Sweden Valley by a silver prospector?

A. The Coudersport Ice Mine.

Q. What percentage of Pennsylvania soil is glacial in nature?

A. Twenty-two percent.

Q. What are the tunnels off the main vertical shaft of a coal mine called?

A. Gangways.

Q. The gray squirrel commonly seen in Pennsylvania is called by what nickname?

A. "Bushytail" squirrel.

Q. What was the name of Philadelphian Dr. Coleman Sellers's 1860 invention, the first to utilize moving photographs?

A. Kinematoscope.

Q. By 1750, Reading was noted as a major colonial collecting and shipping point for what grain?

A. Wheat.

Q. What means of propulsion was used to move cars on Pennsylvania's first railroad?

A. Horses.

Q. West Overton-born industrialist Henry Clay Frick for many years controlled what product instrumental in the production of iron and steel?

A. Coke.

Q. What type of aviation equipment was tested for the first time on October 8, 1929, on a Cleveland, Ohio, to Pittsburgh flight?

A. Automatic pilot.

Q. Concordville is the birthplace of what famous dairy product?

A. Cream cheese.

Q. What is the only type of hummingbird found in Pennsylvania?

A. Ruby-throated.

Q. In 1858 Hyman L. Lipman of Philadelphia invented what writing instrument?

A. Pencil with attached eraser.

Q. O. B. Shallenberger of Rochester patented what device enabling accurate measurement of electricity consumption?

A. The electric meter.

Q. What was the most common color of mink pelts produced in Pennsylvania in 1986?

A. Demi-buff.

Q. What resident of Northumberland from 1794 to 1804 discovered oxygen?

A. Joseph Priestley.

Q. Founded in 1812, what is the nation's oldest continually operating institution of sciences?

A. The Academy of Natural Sciences of Philadelphia.

Q. What is the only type of wildcat found in Pennsylvania?

A. Bobcat.

Q. In 1828 the Pennsylvania Horticultural Society became the first organization in the nation to sponsor what type of exhibition?

A. A fruit exhibition.

Q. Where in Pennsylvania were mine shafts in excess of one thousand feet dug during the 1860s in an attempt to "mine oil"?

A. Smethport.

Q. The title "father of photography in America" was given to what Huntington native?

A. Joseph Saxton.

Q. What is Pennsylvania's leading crop?

A. Mushrooms.

Q. What organization formed in Philadelphia in 1840 evolved into the American Association for the Advancement of Science?

A. The American Association of Geologists.

Q. What cave formation discovered near Manns Choice in 1932 is noted for its fossil deposits and unique formation?

A. Coral Caverns.

Q. Benjamin Franklin believed that walking about one's bedroom in the nude helped induce what state?

A. Sleep.

Q. What Pittsburgh botanical garden displays more than 150 varieties of flora, each with a biblical name or reference?

A. Rodef Shalom Biblical Botanical Garden.

Q. What is the official Pennsylvania state flower?

A. Mountain laurel.

Q. What Pittsburgh attraction is called "an amusement park for the mind"?

A. The Carnegie Science Center.

Q. In 1974 what medical college became the first in the nation to admit a blind student?

A. Temple University.

Q. In 1822 Philadelphians John Farr and Abraham Kunzi became the first American pharmacists to produce what fever-reducing drug?

A. Quinine.

Q. York was the birthplace of what variety of apple?

A. The York Imperial.

Q. What Lawrence County company is credited with creating plastic shock-proof handles on hand tools?

A. Old Forge Tools in New Wilmington.

Q. How far does Preque Isle State Park jut into Lake Erie?

A. Seven miles.

Q. What Philadelphia museum was the nation's first museum for children age seven and under?

A. Please Touch Museum for Children.

Q. What facility protects the remnants of a midwestern prairie ecological system extending back six thousand years, containing a stand of blazing star, a rare prairie flower that blooms in July?

A. Jennings Environmental Education System, Slippery Rock.

Q. For what type of ore are the Cornwall Ore Banks known?

A. Magnetite iron ore.

Q. What library at Exton features three thousand volumes about the history of steam power?

A. Thomas Newcomen Library and Museum.

Q. At its peak production of eight thousand tons per day, what Reynoldsville bituminous coal mine was at one time the most productive mine of its type in the world?

A. The Soldier Run Mine.

Q. What geological feature has received the title of "Grand Canyon of Pennsylvania"?

A. Pine Creek Gorge.

Q. At age thirty-four Dr. Charles Glen King, professor at the University of Pittsburgh, discovered what preventative for scurvy and malnutrition?

A. Vitamin C.

Q. In 1796 what kind of bridge was built at Uniontown to span Jacobs Creek, the first of its kind in the United States?

A. A suspension bridge.

Q. What is the Pennsylvania state tree?

A. Hemlock.

Q. Who in 1904 established Pennsylvania's first commercial cultivation of mushrooms?

A. Edward Jacob.

Q. Where is one of the largest standardbred horse breeders in the world?

A. Hanover Shoe Farms, Hanover.

Q. Lake Arthur is part of what state park?

A. Moraine State Park.

Q. Col. Lewis Walker financed the refinement of what invention and in 1913 constructed a factory for its manufacture in his hometown of Meadville?

A. The slide fastener (generally called a zipper).

Q. In 1887 what sound reproduction device was demonstrated for the first time by Emile Berliner at the Franklin Institute in Philadelphia?

A. Disc phonograph record.

Q. Because of its fertile, high-elevation farm land, what county is nicknamed the "Roof Garden of Pennsylvania"?

A. Somerset.

Q. Philadelphian Casper Wistar lent his name to what ornamental flowering vine?

A. The wistaria (often called wisteria).

Q. What is the largest cave in Pennsylvania?

A. Laurel Caverns, Uniontown.

Q. In 1946 engineers from the University of Pennsylvania built what innovative electrical device?

A. The first fully electronic digital computer.

Q. Who directed the first geological survey of Pennsylvania?

A. Henry Rogers.

Q. Where did antislavery politician and physician Dr. Francis Julius LeMoyne construct the nation's first crematory in 1876?

A. Washington, Pennsylvania.

———◆———

Q. At the Land of Little Horses near Gettysburg, visitors are entertained by what smallest breed of horse?

A. Falabella (three feet high at maturity).

———◆———

Q. What is the Pennsylvania state dog?

A. Great Dane.

———◆———

Q. What annual payment is issued to an heir of Baron Steigel, eighteenth-century glassblower, for rent due on property used by the Zion Lutheran Church in Manheim?

A. A single red rose.

———◆———

Q. Under what name did several enterprising "medicine men" bottle and sell Pennsylvania crude oil as a cure-all in the early 1800s?

A. Seneca Oil.

———◆———

Q. Where in 1843 was bituminous coal first used to fire a Pennsylvania blast furnace?

A. Sharon, Mercer County.

———◆———

Q. What is the smallest federally designated wilderness in the nation?

A. Allegheny Islands Wilderness (seven islands totaling 368 acres).

Q. What river has been referred to by artists as "the Currier and Ives of rivers"?

A. The Susquehanna.

Q. On April 29, 1982, what drink was named the official state beverage?

A. Milk.

Q. What household product was invented in 1907 by Irvin and Clarence Scott of Philadelphia?

A. Paper towels.

Q. In the 1860s Julius Sturgis constructed the nation's first factory at Lititz for the manufacture of what food item?

A. Pretzels.

Q. What was unusual about the first automobile produced by the Pullman Motor Company of York County?

A. It featured six wheels.

Q. At their peak in the mid-1800s, how many saltworks existed along the Conemaugh River in the vicinity of Saltsburg?

A. Twenty-one.

Q. What eastern Pennsylvania wildlife sanctuary contains 150 acres of virgin woods with trees estimated to be eight hundred years old?

A. Woodbourne Wildlife Sanctuary.

Q. What nickname has been given to Indiana County?

A. "A Christmas Tree Capital of the World."

Q. Discovered in 1871, what is Pennsylvania's oldest operating commercial cave?

A. Crystal Cave (near Kutztown).

Q. Pennsylvania is the only place in the world where all six species of what family of fish are found?

A. Pike.

Q. What bird did Benjamin Franklin suggest as the national bird?

A. Wild turkey.

Q. A vaccine for humans for the prevention of what type of deadly fever was announced in Philadelphia on April 28, 1932?

A. Yellow fever.

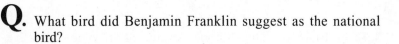

Q. An accident at what Pennsylvania nuclear power plant in 1979 sent shock waves and raised questions of safety throughout the industry?

A. Three Mile Island.

Q. In what county in 1878 was the first well drilled exclusively for gas production?

A. Westmoreland.

Q. The Archbald Pothole, measuring thirty-eight feet in depth and forty-two in diameter, was created by what natural phenomenon?

A. Glacial waterfalls.

Q. In the 1800s, what hunter of the Tunkhannock is credited with having killed some nineteen hundred deer?

A. John McHenry.

Q. Where in 1870 did Henry R. Heyl debut his moving picture invention called a phasmatrope?

A. Philadelphia Academy of Music.

Q. What type of beneficial European ground cover was introduced to Pennsylvania farmers around 1790?

A. Red clover.

Q. Jenners Township in Somerset County was named for what famous English doctor?

A. Dr. Edward Jenner, developer of the smallpox vaccine.

Q. What poisonous snake is most commonly found in Pennsylvania?

A. Copperhead.

Q. Pittsburgh industrialist Phillip Dressler is known for what invention?

A. Tunnel kilns.

Q. James Henry Mitchell of Philadelphia designed a machine for the manufacture of what taste treat in the 1890s?

A. Fig newtons.

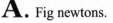

Q. What is the largest remaining tidal wetland in Pennsylvania?

A. Tinicum National Environmental Center, Essington.

Q. Pennsylvanian Rev. Alexander Forsythe revolutionized the firearms industry with what invention in the early 1800s?

A. Percussion cap.

Q. In 1782, what Philadelphian built a pendulum that made clocks more accurate?

A. David Rittenhouse.

Q. Musician Fred Waring used acquired engineering know-how to perfect what invention?

A. The Waring food blender.

Q. What county produces 95 percent of the grapes grown in Pennsylvania?

A. Erie County.

Q. Robert Gilmour of Somerset County patented what handy garden hose attachment?

A. Pistol-grip spray nozzle.

Q. What highly acclaimed horticultural display near Kennett Square features eleven thousand different kinds of plants?

A. Longwood Gardens.

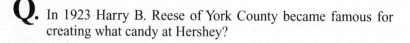

Q. In 1923 Harry B. Reese of York County became famous for creating what candy at Hershey?

A. Reese's Peanut Butter Cup.

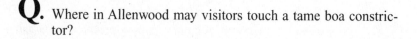

Q. What is the official Pennsylvania state fish?

A. Brook trout.

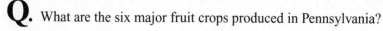

Q. Where in Allenwood may visitors touch a tame boa constrictor?

A. Clyde Peeling's Reptiland.

Q. What eighteenth-century Philadelphia physician was the first to perform autopsies in America?

A. Dr. Thomas Cadwalader.

Q. Encompassing a five-county area in the Allegheny foothills of southwestern Pennsylvania, what region yields vacationers a wide variety of outdoor experiences?

A. Laurel Highlands.

Q. What are the six major fruit crops produced in Pennsylvania?

A. Apples, peaches, pears, sweet cherries, tart cherries, and grapes.

Q. Established in 1824, what Pennsylvania institution of applied sciences and mechanical arts became the first of its kind in the United States?

A. The Franklin Institute.

Q. Where on April 17, 1861, was the Commonwealth's first recorded oil well fire?

A. Rouseville.

Q. What cave complex was discovered in Huntingdon County in 1930 during the construction of U.S. Highway 22?

A. Lincoln Caverns.

Q. Somerset County is Pennsylvania's leading producer of what grain?

A. Oats.

Q. Along what Pennsylvania pioneer road was the first oil pipeline constructed to the Atlantic seaboard?

A. The Coudersport-Jersey Shore Turnpike.

Q. The first municipal water pumping system in the colonies has been restored at what location?

A. Eighteenth-Century Industrial Quarter, Bethlehem.

Q. Though Benjamin Franklin created the first bifocals in 1784, what Philadelphian developed the one-piece bifocal lens by fusing the top and bottom pieces in 1906?

A. John L. Borsch.

Q. What type of building access was invented by Philadelphian Theophilus Van Kannel in 1888?

A. Revolving door.

Q. In 1853 Samuel Wetherill opened at Bethlehem the nation's first mill to extract what metal from calamine ore?

A. Zinc.

Q. What Lawrence County native received international recognition for work with the deaf?

A. Louise Treadwell Tracey.

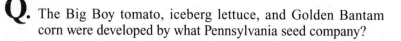

Q. The state's record high temperature of 111° on July 9–10, 1936, occurred in what community?

A. Phoenixville.

Q. The Big Boy tomato, iceberg lettuce, and Golden Bantam corn were developed by what Pennsylvania seed company?

A. W. Attlee Burpee Company.

Q. In a 1757 treatise Benjamin Franklin proposed that electricity be used in the treatment of what type of patients?

A. Paralytics.

Q. What is the largest variety of owl found in the Commonwealth?

A. Great horned owl.

Q. What famous explorer and discoverer of the North Pole was born in Cresson in 1856?

A. Robert Edwin Peary.

Q. The Children's Hospital of Philadelphia witnessed America's first successful operation of what type in 1974?

A. Separation of siamese twins (one-year-old Clara and Altagracia Rodriguez).

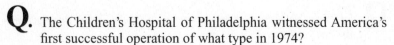

Q. What revolutionary train engine was first track tested at Erie on November 15, 1948?

A. Gas turbine electric locomotive.

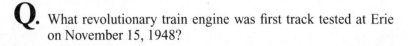

Q. In 1870 Gen. Benjamin Chew Tilghman of Philadelphia came up with what process to clean stone?

A. Sandblasting.

Q. Where was the first supertanker constructed?

A. Sun Ship Yard, Delaware County.

Q. Silver Thread Falls is on what stream?

A. Dingman's Creek.

Q. The binocular microscope was developed by what Philadelphian?

A. Frederic Eugene Ives.

Q. What eighteenth-century Pennsylvanian is known as "the Father of Astronomy"?

A. David Rittenhouse.

◆

Q. The Philadelphia Zoo was the first in the world to house what animal community?

A. A prairie dog village.

◆

Q. What facility operated by the Pennsylvania Fish and Boat Commission propagates mountain trout?

A. Reynoldsdale Fish Cultural Station, near Bedford.

◆

Q. What is the official Pennsylvania state insect?

A. Firefly.

◆

Q. On April 10, 1892, what organization dedicated to combating a deadly lung disease was formed in Philadelphia?

A. Pennsylvania Society for the Prevention of Tuberculosis.

◆

Q. What nineteenth-century Philadelphian was noted for his studies of astigmatism and colorblindness?

A. Isaac Hayes.

◆

Q. In 1976 what name was given to an infectious respiratory illness contracted by several persons attending a convention in Philadelphia?

A. Legionnaires' disease (because it struck at an American Legion convention).

Q. What type of identification system was first used by John Audubon to keep track of a brood of phoebes on his Mill Grove farm?

A. Banding with silver wire and tags.

———◆———

Q. Charles Lennig of Philadelphia created what cleaning agent in 1847?

A. Bleaching powder (chlorine).

———◆———

Q. What Huntingdon-born scientist and inventor built the world's first dynamo?

A. John Saxton.

———◆———

Q. Germantown native Charles Goodyear Jr. revolutionized shoe making by introducing what piece of equipment to the industry?

A. Howe's sewing machine.

———◆———

Q. Fearing ridicule, Benjamin Franklin conducted in private what now-famous test on June 15, 1752?

A. The electrical kite experiment.

———◆———

Q. Ricketts Glen State Park is adorned by how many waterfalls?

A. Thirty-three.

———◆———

Q. Gimbel's of Philadelphia was the first store in America to use what mode of moving customers from floor to floor?

A. Escalator.

Q. On October 16, 1839, from what item did Joseph Saxon construct a camera that took the first heliograph in the nation?

A. A cigar box.

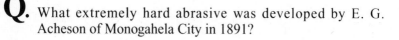

Q. What extremely hard abrasive was developed by E. G. Acheson of Monogahela City in 1891?

A. Carborundum (silicon carbide).

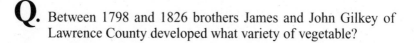

Q. Called "the Father of America's Water-Works," what engineer/architect designed Philadelphia's first municipal water system?

A. Benjamin H. Latrobe.

Q. Between 1798 and 1826 brothers James and John Gilkey of Lawrence County developed what variety of vegetable?

A. Neshannock potato.

Q. Alumnus Lee Iacocca spearheaded the Iacocca Institute at what major research university?

A. Lehigh.

Q. What 1941 structure sharply improved attendance at the Philadelphia Zoo?

A. The Elephant House (which used barless enclosures).

Q. Covering 8,579 acres, what Philadelphia park is the world's largest landscaped city park?

A. Fairmount Park.